LOVE SEEKER

Part Two

Lost

Barbara Ann Quinlan

To Zohar
with love le'olam…

Author's Note

This book is a memoir and as the dictionary will tell you, a memoir is a historical account or biography written from personal knowledge. This memoir is my memoir and so is written with and from my personal knowledge. Where that differs from the historical record, as decided on, or written, by others, then I can only say, that's not how I recall it.

Where it differs from your own knowledge, should you be in or near to my life, or the situations I describe, then again, I can but say, we see from our own eyes.

Being my present recollections of experiences, tempered by the passing of time, I have no doubt that some details may vary from supposed fact. Some names and characteristics may have been changed, some events compressed, and some dialogue recreated. All I can offer is that despite memory being fickle, I have told no lies, nor included any statements that I believe to be untrue. I offer no hurt, nor malice.

I am and always have been a seeker of Love and so I only offer that within these pages. That you may read them and love them for what they are. A story.

My story.

Barbara
New York City
2021

Chapter Eight — Spark

The pinnacle of ecstasy was all too quickly followed by despair, as I awoke one morning to find my face was half-frozen once again. How could it have returned, this dreadful malady that made my life as an actor more and more implausible? Especially while I was enjoying every day as never before, exploring the world I once thought I knew so well now seen from a new perspective, the heaven within.

I was no longer afraid of discovering some dreadful hidden aspect of myself. I had met my true self, ever present within and could commune with it at my leisure.

Even so, preparing my solo performance was a stressful affair. It required me to reach deep into the recesses of my own darkness and its lingering shadows to bring forth a creation; a dramatic portrait that I hoped would show the artful journey of a soul's transformation as I played the anima, the animus, and finally the androgynous. It all led up to the last line spoken, "I have seen the hell of women down there and I shall be free to possess the truth in one body and one soul!"

I found the courage to fight off the paralysis. My family rallied around me in support, willing to take extraordinary steps to aid in the rescue. I journeyed every weekend for treatments with Dr. Siegfried Kanauel, who had moved to a lovely quiet villa just outside Tecate, Mexico. Each of my brothers and my father took turns driving me. I remember having to cover that side of my face with a veil as I looked out the car window to protect my eye from the glaring sun, because the eyelid did not close. I was very touched by the kindness of each of them giving their time to help me in this way.

One day my brother John and I arrived to find the doctor's office door closed. I knew immediately something was wrong. A woman told me that Dr. Kanauel had a stroke in the night. He would not be able to help me that day. Feebly and futilely, I asked when he might be available again.

She regarded me sadly and said, "I don't know."

John and I took a walk together in the garden before leaving. I remembered when Kanauel had seen John on an earlier visit and he commented, "He is the one most like you." I supposed he meant the rabble-rouser part. I was weeping gently all the while we strolled, in agony over so many things: that my beloved doctor had fallen ill, that I didn't know if I would ever see him again—this great man to whom I owed so much—and the helplessness I now felt wondering where I would find help. I fished out of my pants pocket the last squeeze bottle of Kanauel's tincture. It was half full. Then I remembered hearing that Kanauel's wife had cured herself of polio by fasting. "That's what I'll do," I thought to myself. "I'll have to try anyway."

The next day I began the fast. I started by quartering oranges and sucking out the juicy flesh from each piece. Water was my only other sustenance. After 11 days I couldn't bear the sight of an orange, so I stuck to water only, except for tiny measured drops of the tincture.

By the 15th day I began to notice slight movement developing. Then each ensuing day, I noticed a little more. I pressed on for 22 days, until it seemed unwise to continue. I was already slender when I began the fast and had lost 22 pounds in the process. I regained much but not yet all of my facial mobility.

Happily, I got word that Kanauel was back on his feet and able to see me. I decided to go and see him one last time to thank him for his great kindness. I did not want him to spend energy on me that he now needed for himself. On this last visit I told him that while he was sick, I imagined him curing himself, pulling himself out of it from within. He said, "In the end that is what we all must do, heal ourselves." I remain indebted to him for his profound example of healing through love. Instruments and medicine are not enough. Intent is everything!

Shortly thereafter, while attending a discourse at Larchmont Hall, I noticed a man seemingly stroking the halo of his young son's head in a circular motion. Then later, as we crossed each other's paths in the hallway, he stopped me in my tracks and pointing to my face, he said, "I can help you with that." Turns out he was Zion, a highly celebrated acupuncturist from Taiwan, currently teaching the western doctors at UCLA. Acupuncture had helped forestall it once before, perhaps it could help now? I gratefully accepted his offer. He began treating me three times a week for free. Interesting how so many doctors treated me without charge. I was very grateful, though I never knew why he did it, other than kindness. Or was it professional courtesy perhaps? Later I would have the chance to pay it back and followed suit.

Zion's needles miraculously did the trick, and I was fully cured! Years later a maxillofacial surgeon, who was both a patient and a friend of my mine, remarked, "You are the only one I've ever met or know of who has been cured of Bell's Palsy three times. It's very unusual, but these days the highest cure rate comes from a combination of meditation and acupuncture."

Meanwhile, Ossetynski was still unraveled by the thought that I had returned from Poland but with an experience unknown by either him or any of his students. No work in his class had brought forth any such experience. He was also considerably annoyed over the fact that I had recently received and was practicing the gift. He needed to get his hands on something new, something original that he could present in Warsaw, so he asked me for a suggestion.

I told him that Spark was working on something, a play he called Crazy Mary. I asked Spark to send a copy of the script to him to review. It was unusual, and O was intrigued. Could he make something out of it worthy to present in Poland? He asked me to invite Spark down to work with the group and see what we could do with this rather bizarre play he'd written. Spark was free as a bird, having just divorced his first wife, nothing controlling him or his time. He was anxious for a chance to work in theater and possibly see his project come to life, so he agreed to come to Hollywood and work with us.

Initially the plan was for Spark to stay at my place. I was excited to finally have a chance to share with him my newfound peace. I was sure he would be receptive. After all, we had shared so much over the years. I was full of glee over my recent discovery and anxious to tell anyone who would listen. Surely Spark would be interested. How could he not be? He, who used to fast for three days on brown rice before ingesting three tabs of Grateful Dead windowpane acid. I had always assumed he was getting as high as he could to discover as much as he could in that altered state. If not seeking the Truth, what could his purpose have been?

Spark arrived that spring, shortly after I had recovered from the palsy. His embrace was as genuine and enthusiastic as it has always been. Skinny as ever, his well-worn jeans barely clung to his hips. That evening we played together for a brief while to the brink of intercourse but his member was just too large for me to contain, and he had not yet learned to work shallow. But he was pleased to be with me and anxious to get started on his rather complicated play. It involved intense prose, primarily exulting darkness, to be chanted while the actors moved along a vortex pattern painted on the floor.

Honestly, I was hard pressed to be supportive of its content, let alone work on it. He and I were diametrically opposed. I tried to tell him about the magnificent experience I was discovering within me, blatantly describing the beautiful sense of bliss I bathed in.

He rejected it as improbable if not entirely impossible. Never mind that it was me, his lifelong friend and confidante, who was delivering the news. If I had said, "I know of a good place to get some great pizza," we would have been on our way. Or, "There is a profound art film I want you to see." No problem. But that there was an endless peace waiting for him to experience within himself—not interested. Not even given a second thought. He all but declared himself devoted to the lord of darkness. There was a very strange moment in the heat of our discussion when I saw a demonic mask wash over his face. It nearly made me gasp! After that, he stayed at Susan's.

I took pride in being a struggling artist. I worked hard in the studio and still supported myself working in restaurants. I never had much money. If I had it, I spent it. I once heard someone say, "I hate the thought of dying with money in the bank!"

I passed up several opportunities to hear the Teacher speak in person. I had this idea that if he saw me, he might realize that a mistake had been made. His gift was the answer to my lifelong prayer, yet having finally received it I felt unworthy in the face of its majesty.

**

When I was fifteen, I had one of my most disturbing dreams. I was on the shore of a sea, long enough after sunset for the darkening sky to cast its shadow upon the earth. I quickly noticed I was not alone on the beach. In the distance, a hooded faceless figure, shrouded in gray, was beckoning me to follow, and I felt compelled to do so. I was led to a mansion, which I entered with great apprehension. The walls and trimmings were all in fine mahogany, and the rooms were dimly lit. I found myself in a grand room where a long narrow pool of dark water, that cast no reflection, was placed in the center of the floor.

There was a balcony above at one end, the full width of the room. It was filled with barely living bodies, severely maimed and brutally tortured, hacked off limbs, some skinned alive, all pathetic victims of the evil Master of the mansion. When he became aware of my presence, I was terrified at first, until it became clear that he was not concerned as to my whereabouts. And worse, there was the strange sensation that I was him. I woke in deep despair. It would be nearly a decade before I could look in a mirror without seeing his eyes staring back at me! In fact, it was only after I received the gift that I finally felt free of him.

I have always wondered about the difference between the sadikim and the kadoshim (Hebrew for the saints and the holy ones). I figured sainthood could only be certain when the last breath is drawn. But the holy ones, who were they? And which, if either, might I ever become? I was certainly not one of holy ones. I surmised that they must be those returning to life already sanctified. So then the saints would be the ones who worked on it and won!

**

I was now in a pristine state of love and dreamy contentment in the gentle transformation that softened the heart. Then a vulture-like guy named Bart swept down upon me. He was tall, slender, and handsome. I was quickly taken in. How wonderful, a new man in the midst of all this love. However, it wasn't love he was after or even capable of for that matter. I would soon see that he swept up any tender newbies he could find, playing off the peace/love thing for his own selfish satisfaction, but not until I'd gone home with him.

As I laid next to him, waiting for him to make his move, my loins burned with passion for him, until it turned out that his move was a violent slap across my face, and it didn't get any better from there. How was I attracted to those so incapable of true intimacy? Not just attracted, guaranteed I would fall in love with them! I let him dangle me mercilessly. I was in love and so quite vulnerable. Every night after we'd been together, he'd show up with another woman at the hall, presumably to prove to me that I meant nothing to him. I prayed that he would fall off a cliff somewhere, and eventually he did fall out of my life.

The one thing I took from Bart was a brief introduction to macrobiotics. He mentioned it vaguely, and I pursued the study of it. I started with the 7th regime, which required a ten-day fast on organically grown, short-grain brown rice and very little water or bancha tea (roasted twig tea). Then I would have rice cream for breakfast with homemade gomasio dusted over the top, but no sugar, no caffeine, no citrus fruits, no products grown outside of the immediate area, and no red meat.

Vegetables were required to be well cooked, and everything was measured in an attempt to balance the yin and yang. I became a complete vegetarian for several years, though the diet did not require it. I felt powerful on that diet. I only needed to sleep four hours a night and woke entirely refreshed. It became my reset button. Whenever serious illness threatened, I returned to the 7th regime until I became well again. Unfortunately, such austerity brought with it an unhealthy arrogance that did not help my inner growth.

However, it was the perfect time for me to study Choy Li Fut Kung Fu, a fight style made famous by Bruce Lee. I fell in love with it the first time I saw someone performing it as he walked down Hollywood Boulevard. He looked like a dancing monkey.

"What are you doing?" I asked.

"It's Kung Fu, a very special style," he responded. He took me to his Sifu, who happily accepted me as his second woman student among thirty men.

We were all required to be strict vegetarians, because it is thought that meat eaters tend to be more impatient and quicker to anger. This fight style is so powerful, you are first taught to avoid conflict at all costs, until you cannot avoid it, and then God help your opponent! Having already studied Tai Chi, Kathakali, Dynamic Hatha Yoga, and several other Asian disciplines, I was well prepared to take on this training. What with the recent Manson murders and now the Hillside Strangler lurking, I wanted to able to defend myself and my children, should I ever have any.

The Sifu said that you would know it was sinking in when it shows up in your dreams. For me this happened very quickly. I found that this work gave me an inner sense of fortitude. I became more and more fearless, which appealed to me greatly. In class each strike was repeated a hundred times and then on to the next. I quickly mastered a speed and force that made my arms seem invisible. The 15-minute warm up involved standing firm on the various "horse" poses. Last came the twist horse, a crouching twisted stance that made my knees shake almost uncontrollably. At that point I found myself praying, "If you want me to learn this art, don't let me fall down. If I fall, I will leave and not come back!" I never fell.

**

There would only be a few more lovers, however brief, from among those who had received the gift. Once, I met someone when I'd flown to Miami to see the Teacher. A hurricane was approaching, and while all the residents were

9

taping up their windows, we got word to go north to Orlando where it was believed we would be safe. A guy pulled his car up to the sidewalk and asked if I needed a ride. I recognized him, though I didn't know his name. He was clean cut, good looking, and had a nice car, so I hopped in, and off we went!

That night we made love, and in the morning, he presented me with a beautiful blue brocade silk dress that fit perfectly. I can't imagine where he got it, unless from the gift shop of the hotel (doubtful, it was too beautiful). I put it on with delight, and off to the program we went.

The event was held in an open field. The clouds resembled the inside of a mixing bowl with all the beaten egg whites stuck to the sides. I began wandering alone around the field, searching for a ditch I could lay my body in if the hurricane hit.

As I looked, I began to think of my parents. How would they feel if I died here? I had heard that when a hurricane hits it can drive a straw straight through your body, and there was plenty of straw on the ground. Then it struck me that if I died that day, the only one I would be accountable to would be God. My parents would be okay. And God would not ask me what they thought of me or if they approved of my life. It would be: what did I think about what I'd done with my life? Somehow, I felt settled by these thoughts. The hurricane passed us by, and the Teacher gave another brilliant discourse, and I would never be with that boy again. He had been so sweet and kind. I was sorry to see the pained confusion in his eyes when I was leaving. I kept the beautiful dress and went on my way.

Then there was the minor movie star. He was definitely gorgeous, tall, broad shouldered, and specialized in appearing sensitive and sincere. That was as good as his acting got until many years later.

He invited me to visit him while on a short stay at the Chateau Marmont on Sunset. He picked me up and carried me up the stairs to his bedroom.

"This must be what it is like to be romanced by the Hulk," I thought silently. Soon I realized he was just too big for me.

Lastly there was a guy I saw once in a crowd of 5,000 at an event with the Teacher. He was tall, thin, somewhat handsome, and had an aloof air, backed by a perplexing wind that seemed to push him as a breeze of despair blew across his face. I asked my girlfriend Ronnie who he was as he strode by.

"Oh, that's so-and-so," she said. "He's married to a woman who has two kids. He has just written his first book. It's making him famous around the world. All I heard was, "He's married," and I didn't give him a second thought for decades.

Chapter Nine — Wiesław

The time for my return to Poland was fast approaching. Nearly two years had passed, and I was now holding the key that I thought I could use to escape the grave. Free of any trace of doubt, I was still gestating within the miraculous tabernacle that housed my soul, the soul I had come to love, with a heart now beating like the wings of a young bird about to take flight.

I was anxious to tell my friends, especially Wiesław, that I had found the treasure of life. A love so perfect and so bright, it dispels darkness.

I left for Europe two months before the others; I would join them in Warsaw. Emmanuelle had invited me to stay in the apartment she was sharing with her sister and brother-in-law, both professors at the Sorbonne. A young male student of theirs was staying as well. Large enough for me to have a small room of my own, it was located in Montparnasse, adjacent to the flat where Jean Paul Sartre was living with Simone. Had I ever been interested in existentialism I might have crossed the corner to meet them, but I was not and did not.

Emmanuelle and Chloe were both shocked to hear that I had taken the gift from the Teacher. They knew me to be entirely independent. My inability to join in had kept me out of ensemble work. What had become of me? They seemed disappointed, as if I had somehow let them down.

Really? I thought. Even you two, my dearest and closest girlfriends, writing it off without as much as a moment's consideration? They were more preoccupied with what they thought was the Teacher's identity than what he might have shown me. Chloe asked me, "If you knew you were going to die in ten minutes, what would you do?"

Without a second's hesitation I responded, "I would go within." My answer seemed to stump them. However, our love for one another in no way subsided. I did not need them to believe in anything, though I did wish they knew for themselves.

I sat at the edge of a mattress on the floor that was my bed, rolling a joint of crumbled hash-laced tobacco. Yes, I still smoked both cigarettes and pot, despite that fact that I was now practicing the gift, concept after concept broken. Pot was difficult to come by in Paris, but hash was plentiful. Jean did not smoke except for the occasional Gauloises (French cigarette), and I wanted a joint before he arrived. Amazing how even cottonmouth could be remedied within. I need never be thirsty again, I thought.

It was interesting how many people tried to point out the idea that perfection and smoking didn't go together. I guess it was their attempt to negate the validity of the experience I claimed to be having. Their concepts and judgment impeded their understanding. Oh, I did feel guilty about smoking anything, because I too suffered from my ideals regarding perfection.

As for Jean, I was thrilled to be with him again. So happy that he still wanted me as much as I wanted him. We picked up where we left off. Our passion for each other was still burning hot. Our steps were still in synch as we strode down the streets of Paris.

Emmanuelle's parents owned a beautiful country home outside Paris. She invited Chloe, Jean, and me to join her there for the weekend before I left for Warsaw. It was the only time I would meet her kind parents.

At my request, Emmanuelle and Chloe made a tarte aux pommes (apple tart) as I watched, anxious to learn this French art de cuisine. That night, Jean and I escaped into the meadow, laying together in the tall grasses where we might make love hidden by the nature. And then along wobbled a porcupine! I had never seen one before and wanted to touch it.

Jean grabbed my hand. "C'est piqûre!" ("It stings!") he cautioned.

The next morning, I awoke to find Jean gone. I raced downstairs to the kitchen where Emmanuelle was standing. "Where's Jean?" I asked.

"He left," she stated flatly.

"You didn't think to come and get me?" I was miffed.

"If he wants to leave, is it not his prerogative?"

I flashed her an annoyed look as I picked up my knapsack and ran out the door after him.

I was panting heavily when I arrived at the local train stop. Feverishly paying for a ticket, I hopped on the train at the very last moment. And there was Jean, sitting morosely on a pull-down bench at the back of the wagon.

He feigned annoyance, "Oh, mais c'est pas vrai!" ("Oh, but it isn't true!")

I was too furious to see his relief that I'd come. I dropped my bag, pushed down the seat next to him, and spun around in such a huff that I didn't notice that the

14

spring seat had popped back up against the wall. Soon my angry ass was slammed down hard against the floor. The damage to my coccyx bone was severe and the pain instantaneous.

"Mais qu'est que tu fait?" ("But what are you doing?") Jean asked as he picked me up off the floor.

"Qu'est que tu fait? Pourquoi m'as tu quitté?" ("What are you doing? Why did you leave me?"). I was too self-absorbed to understand what my love might be feeling. Perhaps he was growing more and more attached to me, in love with a young woman he knew would never be able to stay.

I went back with Jean to his place that night. It was a small one-room flat in L'Opera. The walls were filled floor to ceiling with polished dark wood bookshelves stacked with philosophy books. There was a mattress on the floor that served as the bed. We wanted to make love, but I was in so much pain I almost gave up. Then I rolled over, and he came into me from behind. The ecstatic pleasure overrode the pain, and we both came melting into one another's arms. How would I ever be able to let go of him? I wondered silently in the dark.

The next day I was back at Emmanuelle's in Paris. It would be two weeks before I could get up off the bed, unaided. She kindly helped me. Thankfully I was repaired by the time I needed to leave for Warsaw. Jean accompanied me to the train station. There was no need for tearful goodbyes this time, as we knew I'd be back after the work.

Once again, I boarded the Orient Express for Warsaw. Ossetynski, Susan, Roger, and the others had already arrived just before me. I was anxious about the performance that I would soon be giving at the Instytut Kultury. However, I was excited about my plan to return to Wrocław afterwards and have a chance to tell Wiesław about the gift! At last I could return to him with something of great value, as he had already given me so much.

Meanwhile, O and I were not on good terms. As I was still practicing macrobiotics, I had arrived in Poland with ten pounds of organically grown short-grain brown rice. Grandma Domanska allowed me to prepare it in her kitchen. It was difficult enough refusing the gracious hospitality of the Poles, whose many homes we were privileged to visit, but when I took the rice with me into a restaurant for lunch with O and ordered only sautéed mushrooms to put on top, he was outraged.

"You are a pig!" he declared in disgust, nearly spitting as he spoke. He had never forgiven me for running off to study with Grotowski, that I showed more respect for Grot than for him, that I had taken the gift and was practicing it, and finally that I was, in his eyes, not as dedicated to acting as he had always hoped I would be.

He believed I was the most talented of his students, and so perhaps he thought my fame would bring him fame. But I just couldn't take it seriously anymore. After six years of arduous study, I no longer longed for fame. Oh, I would always be an actor, out alone. I suppose he thought I never loved him. Actually, I am indebted to him even now. I hold him in my heart with deep respect for all he taught me. It was worth every drop of sweat and tears. I did love that old man. Perhaps not in the way he wished, but in a way that stays with me today.

The evening of our performances soon arrived. I was almost catatonic from nerves. I had worked over a year and

16

a half on this piece I was about to perform, and suddenly I was convinced I couldn't do it.

Ossetynski was anxious to show the variety of exercises he'd developed with us and our proficiency at performing them. He wore us out with leaping frogs and screaming monkeys. We each did our best to be fully engaged. At his command we performed. We wanted to please him, to do well, and to show our respect for him. Then when the demonstration was finished, he surprised me by announcing that my performance was up next.

The plan had been that Roger's performance of The Mad Man and the Nun, which he would be performing in Polish, would follow immediately after the exercises. I had managed to bring my solo piece down to just over half an hour. I had carefully sculpted each of the three characters, leaving some room to breathe new life and movement into them each time I practiced the performance so that they would not become stale. I knew what I was doing. I was well prepared.

But now, when he called my name, I froze in place, as if completely paralyzed and barely able to breathe! Susan was standing behind me, and she knew what to do. With both of her hands against my back, she shoved me onto the performance floor!

The proscenium arch rose instantly though invisibly between myself and the audience, and an extraordinary performance began. All of the characters I had so carefully created came to life as if I was not there. I was overtaken by creative ecstasy. When I finished, I found myself crouched against the back wall, dazed and wondering what had just happened, as thunderous applause rang through the hall.

In the morning, I packed my bags and prepared to leave Warsaw without a word of goodbye to O. I swore Susan to secrecy, just long enough to facilitate my escape. She had been staying with me at the Domanska's. I kissed and hugged them all, then took a cab to the airport, where I boarded the first plane to Wrocław. It must have been in service since WWII, because the entire cabin shook and rattled all the way there, as if the inside was not actually attached to the outside shell of the plane. I prayed continuously, considering that this might be some sort of punishment for leaving Ossetynski so thoughtlessly.

Ossetynski was kind enough to have settled my lodgings in Wrocław long before I left. This time it was with an old friend of his, presumably from the Polish army and his family. It was obvious that Ossetynski was well respected throughout Poland, perhaps even greatly loved if not admired as a hero. It seems no one could say no to him, but then again he knew how to ask.

My host had been captured by the Nazis and placed in prison. An SS sergeant hung him from the ceiling by his ankles and his wrists for days before he cut him down. Only after he bought his new home did he discover that the previous owner was that same SS sergeant who left him with a lame gait for the rest of his life. It was in the basement of that very house that the sergeant and his entire family killed themselves when the Germans lost the war. Amazing how fate turns.

They picked me up from the airport and took me to their home just at the country edge of Wrocław. It was a beautiful old Manor House, complete with a veranda and a wonderful solarium. All the wood trimmings were in dark mahogany. I was given a lovely room to stay in. They were very gracious and good to me. After a night's rest I headed out for The Theater Laboratory in the morning to find Wiesław and tell him the wonderful news.

I woke early to practice, had my usual brown rice and tea for breakfast, then headed into town. The central square was saturated in the morning light. I found my way to the theatre door and knocked excitedly before opening it. The entryway seemed dark, despite the fact that light was seeping through the thresholds of the front offices.

Three shadowy figures quickly appeared to greet me. Soon I recognized that Ludwig Flagen was among them. I had barely gotten out the words that I was looking for Wiesław when a sudden sense of gloom filled the air.

One of them gently touched my shoulder and spoke two words that I could not understand. "He's dead."

What language was this? Surely, I had not heard correctly.

Then even more gently, he said, "He was buried early today."

I started to slip deeper into shock. This is not possible I thought. "What are you saying? What are you talking about?" I demanded, incredulously.

Without trying to convince me, another man stepped forward and handed me a piece of paper saying, "Here, he left this for you." It was a note asking me to come to Zakopane to meet him. He would wait for me in the mountain village of his childhood. He had been studying Hinduism and was anxious to see me.

My protests were met with deeply knowing glances. There were no words. They could only silently support me as I sank, inconsolable. Short on facts and unable to answer my increasingly demanding interrogation, someone took me to Wiesław's aunt.

I found myself standing in a beautiful old townhouse flat. His aunt wore the mark of mourning on her face. Looking back, it was at that very moment I knew it was true. Still I desperately demanded an explanation. He had gone back to the village of his childhood in the mountains of Zakopane. Emmanuelle had already informed him that I was coming and I had taken the gift. He was researching it while he waited for me.

The pilot was out on the small gas water heater that hung above the tub, unnoticed by Wiesław. In Poland there was no scent added to the odorless natural gas. That meant one would not know if gas was escaping. Wiesław shut the bathroom door behind him, uncapped a bottle of beer with his teeth, and sank himself into the cold bath, as was his custom since the death of his mother. There he fell into a deep deathlike sleep, the gas poisoning him while angels gently wept. He was swept away until finally out of reach.

I wept copiously as it began to sink in. His aunt rushed into my arms. She saw my love for him, and I saw in her face the pain of my heart. His aunt was a very strong woman, yet she stepped back and did not attempt to control my rage. I marched out onto the balcony and I shook my fist at the sky.

"How could you do this?" I cried out. "You let him die without the gift. He who had most deserved it. And I am left here standing so unworthy." There is no justice, I thought. I knew so well the powerful energy that could have saved him. It did not have to happen. Why save me and kill him? No! I cannot accept this! Just then something snapped in me, though I was unaware of it at the time. Nor did I understand the magnitude of its impact.

I continued to rant and rage on the balcony unimpeded until I collapsed. Then the dear young man who had brought me there from The Theater Laboratory encouraged me to get back on my feet, lifting me gently off the floor in his strong kind arms. He was a friend, a few years younger than Wiesław, who was 27 when he died. His kindness and gentleness was like my friend. He took over as my guardian and did not leave my side. I asked for Olaf at some point, but he was away in Yugoslavia.

"Does he know?" I asked.

"I think so," he responded.

"Would you like me to take you there? To his grave?" he pressed softly, a little further.

"Yes, please take me now."

Wiesław had been buried only ten hours before. My walk into the cemetery was surreal. Where was I going? What would I find there? All was a blur until that moment when I stood there over his freshly filled grave, smelling the turned earth.

Why were my arms not long enough to reach him, to pull him out? I was delirious with disillusionment, as the tears poured like rain down my face. "What can I do?" I said aloud, shaking my head in despair.

"Remember him in the light!" the young man said with absolute unwavering assurance.

Ah, but I had already developed my own idea. "I will live double now. I will live for both of us!"

"You want a drink?"

"Oh yes!"

We headed to Palawicz, where I drank brandy and danced into the night, repeatedly toasting to Wiesław's great life! My sweet guardian then took me back to my room, explaining to the family what had happened, as I fell on my bed and cried myself to sleep.

In the morning, I joined them at the dining room table for breakfast without stopping to boil some rice. On the table were fresh strawberries, whipped cream, and sugar. I served myself an ample portion of each and gratefully accepted a cup of coffee. Macrobiotics be damned, macro life begin!

Soon my gallant guardian returned and took me to Wiesław's family. There I sat in his stepmother's salon. She was overwrought with sadness. I remember there was a cute little boy named Tomik. His innocent happiness was remarkable and reminded me of Wiesław. They gave me a beautiful book of Wrocław and a photo of Wiesław as a little boy on his tricycle. I still have both. We cried together for a while, and then I went away with my fury and my memories. I returned to Paris where I could still embrace the ones I loved.

Emmanuelle's sad round eyes quickly welled up with tears when she greeted me at the door of their apartment. She knew. She, too, could say nothing. We rushed over the dark moment to embrace, clinging to the life within us, our hearts still beating in these fearless frail bodies. Over tea, which Emmanuelle had prepared with care, she told me that Jean had already called. Then Emmanuelle looked at me inquisitively as she presented me with a note that Gerald had dropped by.

"Ah yes, Gerald, we worked together on a screenplay he planned to market at the Deauville Festival. I was helping him with the translation," I said to a bewildered Emmanuelle.

I didn't tell her that we'd also had a brief affair and that his lovemaking had been passionate though somehow distanced. But what was he doing here, at Emmanuelle's? I had no desire to rekindle any form of flame with him.

Gerald's note said he'd be stopping by within the next half hour to see if I would go out for coffee. Jean wasn't due to arrive until eight.

Of course, Jean arrived early, just in time to meet Gerald, whom I quickly brushed off and shooed away. Flinging my arms around Jean, I kissed both his cheeks, then paused before his lips and looking deep into his eyes I told him, "Je t'aime!"

Gerald's note said he'd be stopping by within the next half hour to see if I would go out for coffee. Jean wasn't due to arrive until eight.

Of course, Jean arrived early, just in time to meet Gerald, whom I quickly brushed off and shooed away. Flinging my arms around Jean, I kissed both his cheeks, then paused before his lips and looking deep into his eyes I told him, "Je t'aime!"

"Who was that?" he asked in plain English.

"Why, that's Gerald," I answered as if I didn't get the question.

"Je connais son nom, mais qui est-il?" ("I know his name, but who is he?")

Ah, who is he? Without missing a beat, I rambled off the same explanation I'd given Emmanuelle. All the while a flash of intensely burning lovemaking flashed in my mind. But Gerald would later inform me that my lack of pubic hair was a turnoff for him. He preferred a raven's web. I was never in love with him, though I had enjoyed the sex.

Jean made a comment to my story about helping to translate the screenplay. He was silent for some time thereafter as we marched along the boulevards. How did I not know that he knew and was hurt? Surely, he must have guessed that something might have gone on, but as long as I said nothing it wasn't real. Was it?

If only I had given a moment's thought to how Jean might be feeling, even if he was only suspecting something had gone on between Gerald and me. Wiesław's death had made me so much more aware, but of what? We went on with our precious lives.

Here we were, Jean and me together, breathing the same air, and I longed for nothing else.

Then the time for parting came again. Jean and Emmanuelle took me to the station. Emmanuelle took wonderful photos of us, the elegant lovers parting. We sat in the station café for a while, playing together in a booth. I was returning to Los Angeles. I was leaving Jean, though I wanted to stay with him. How would I have fit myself into his world? What was driving me so hard was that, though I could hear my heart, I would not listen to it! Of course, I promised to write him, insisting that we would be together again, looking for a trace of belief in his eyes. If I had known that this goodbye would be the last, would I still have said it?

The tears streamed down my face. Jean tried to brush them away. The longing to stay became almost unbearable.

Decades later I would still want to see his face, to once more feel our footsteps as we marched along the boulevards and into the alleys.

Chapter Ten — Mercy

I returned to L.A., ostensibly to build a career as an actor while waiting on tables. Ah, the casting-couch invitations that would come! After all I had gone through to gain my skill, I wasn't about to lie down for anyone.

Before leaving for Europe I had been working at a German restaurant called the "Lowenbrau Keller". It was a gorgeous tribute to authentic German architecture and cooking. The owner had been kind enough to let me come back to work when I returned, even though they had already hired someone in my place—Patricia from Alabama, Patty for short.

I remember the first moment I saw her. She was doing some prep work for the chef. Patty was about a year older than me, a dark-haired southern beauty with bright hazel eyes, and her accent was still intact. Quite friendly, she quickly informed me that she lived with her partner Eli, whom I briefly mistook to be a girl, not realizing that he was Israeli and Eli was a common name for boys. Theirs was quite an unlikely story. Patty had left her family and friends in Alabama, hopped into her new red Camaro, and drove across the country to Sacramento. There she wandered into an Israeli nightclub where Eli was singing. They caught each other's glance immediately, though neither approached the other that first night. Then two nights later Patty went back, and they've been together ever since!

Patty invited me back to her place on the west side of Hollywood. We were only there a few minutes when she picked up the phone and called the next-door neighbor Roni. Two minutes later he was at the door with some pot.

Roni was gorgeous. He had thick dark hair, dark eyes, golden skin, and a beautifully carved face. I was hot for him before we all finished smoking a joint together. He left right after we finished it. As soon as he was gone, I asked Patty about him.

"Oh, he's married to Ronite. They have a new baby."

I tried to put a stop to my feelings immediately. I would've erased him from my memory, were it not that I saw him again and again. He and his stunning wife used to enter the nightclubs like two magnificent dark angels, the purest twin of one another. Still, I wanted him.

I remember the first time he came to the club without Ronite. We were all sitting together at a long banquet table, as was the style in the Greek club. I remember how nervous he was looking back and forth, nursing his drink on the rocks.

When I couldn't take it anymore, I stood up and said, "Excuse me, good evening, I have to leave."

Roni decided he would walk me out the door and in the parking lot, he kissed me. In a second we were deeply entwined in a passionate embrace. How could I avoid him now? I was not used to forsaking such deep desire and he too was overwhelmed.

Then one day he just showed up at my door. I led him up the stairs without saying a word and made love to him passionately, until we were both breathless. Roni was the perfect size for me, tapered so beautifully allowing easy insertion with maximum thrust. He was visibly shocked by his lust and it would soon turn to love.

We began to meet often, any time of the day that we could get free. And there were no words, only passion expressed with such incredibly sweet, smooth, and tender intimacy. Both of us were stunned by the sensuous grasp that held us. Oh, I was still living my life, but he was an unavoidable desire. One day he brought his little baby to my home to meet me. I realized then that he was falling in love with me.

I've never been one for talking during sex. A few "Oh God's" with the occasional tender whispers was natural to me, but vulgarity, no. For me sexuality was an act of intense beauty, a sharing of tactile feelings as well as intent. Our bodies read each other spontaneously. I took lovers who knew what I wanted without words.

But as my father was fond of saying, "Familiarity breeds contempt." Roni began saying things I didn't want to hear while making love. At first it was the occasional, "You bitch." Then, "You're a motherfucker." I did not warn him that this would lead to the end. I interpreted his comments as evidence of his reluctance to be with me, perhaps feeling guilty about Ronite and the baby. We had kept our relationship clandestine.

Eli and Roni were good friends, so Eli and Patty knew and were definitely against me for it, as Ronite and Roni were well loved in the community. Funny how Roni's involvement with me was somehow regarded as less reprehensible than mine with him because it was normal for a man to be unfaithful. I have often underestimated people's need for gossip and in how few hands my secrets could be trusted. That alone might have been another reason I would ultimately back off but not yet.

Patty once said that it was my eyes that had originally attracted her to me. Everyone who knew me or met me was amazed by my exuberance and apparent happiness, my intense energy laced with inescapable joy. Anyone could see it, though very few could understand it. I tried to explain the wonderful gift from the Teacher that allowed me to see the beauty within myself.

I remember one day standing with Patty at the bar in the Lowenbrau Keller, wiping down glasses shortly before the restaurant opened, and causally talking to her about the gift.

"Sounds to me like you're talking about God, and for me that's very personal."

I said nothing more, and we would rarely speak of it again, though she was present many times when I spoke of it to others.

I often felt as if the world was starving, and I knew where there was a silo of grain. I wanted to share it, to tell them they needn't be hungry any more. This lofty vision of life made my behavior even more impalpable. How could I be so blessed and so blasphemous at the same time?

Roni was a barber. He had his own exclusive shop at the edge of Beverly Hills. An excellent hair stylist, he had only recently quit working on women's hair.

"Too much trouble," he said.

He seemed sincerely interested in the idea of being able to access peace within. But if it meant receiving something from anyone other than Moses, it was out of the question for him as a Jew.

"We only follow Moses."

I wanted to ask where Moses was now, but I refrained. Many Israelis took the gift, just not the ones I knew. What image was I sending, I've often wondered?

Roni, searching for a way to spend innocent time together, asked if I rode horses.

"Only once when I was ten."

That was when my friend Becky showed me her horse and asked if I'd like to ride him.

"Sure," I said fearlessly.

Once in the corral she gave me just a few instructions: up on the left, loose with the reins, walk, trot, then canter. I was able to take him through his paces as if I had been riding all my life.

Roni found that story not at all believable, but invited me to join him and his friend for a Sunday morning ride nonetheless.

His closest friend was an Israeli redhead nicknamed Gingi. Neither of them believed that I had only been on a horse once before. As we drove together to the stables, they were making jokes about how I was a seasoned horsewoman just trying to fool them. Who else in their right mind would venture out with two horsemen on a mountain ride?

When we arrived at Griffith Park, I was given a mare named Idaho. Left side up I remembered. Once in the saddle I thought of Caesar's line to the oarsman in Bernard Shaw's play *Anthony and Cleopatra*. I transposed it in my mind and told the horse telepathically, "You're carrying me and my Grace." Before long we were galloping across the vast prairie on our way to the mountainside.

After seeing how I handled myself they were sure I had lied about the number of times I'd been on a horse. All of a sudden Roni turned his horse and started straight up the mountain. I had an overwhelming sense of déjà vu at that moment. Long ago, I thought, I had seen him before on a horse climb straight up the mountainside.

I felt a powerful sense of camaraderie that gave me the courage to follow right behind him up the mountain. The next thing I knew we were walking the horses, hoof over hoof, on the very narrow ridge of the mountaintop. It was a sharp slide down either side. In moments like this, one doesn't dare to show or even feel fear. I made it across the ridge, and we started to head down the mountain. On a small plateau overlooking the valley we stopped to eat the lunch I had brought for us all.

Gingi was a self-declared moralist, highly objecting to Roni's and my sexual relationship but it was obvious that he liked me despite that. I saw him as a kind and gentle man, an image that one day would be destroyed, along with so many others.

One night I agreed to meet Roni at his home in West Hollywood. He tried to take me to their bed but I insisted we use the second room. It was the baby's room but Ronite had gone away for the evening with the child.

As we made love he cried out in a mad whisper, "You are the devil."

I was shocked and repulsed. It meant to me that he saw me as an evil influence in his life. It was completely opposite of what I truly wanted. Though I was not in love with him, I loved him dearly like a brother, but I dropped the brother part for the passion.

I went with my friends, Ronnie and Jonny to see a psychic woman who was living in the Yucca Desert near Palm Springs. They had said amazing things about her, and that she did not charge money but would take a very small donation somehow aroused my interest enough for me to be willing to take the two-and-a-half-hour drive there.

I remember her telling me, "First I'll put my feet in the water. There's a stream here," she said, indicating the floor under her feet, invisible to me. Suddenly she was scratching her nose. "Ooh!" she said, "somebody is there tickling my nose with a feather."

She began, "You're constantly surrounded by 12 American Indians." An absurd term when you think about it, for they are not at all Indians, as Columbus discovered America not India, so they are Native Americans.

I was pleased and somehow not surprised, as I had been aware of them since I was very young, maybe since age five, mostly subconsciously. The awareness floated in my mind but rarely to the surface. Like when I was five and got up in the middle of the night to use the bathroom, but I was afraid to touch the back of the seat for fear a tomahawk would come through my back. I have a birthmark on my spine in the middle of my back. As an adult I heard that birthmarks were the stain of a mortal wound from the past.

Then she said, "Do you know you're with someone now in this life who was your brother in a past life?"

"Yes, I know," I responded.

"And did you know that you were his brother as well?"

I responded, "I think he saved my life."

"You needed saving," she said. "A great wave came and swept you off the deck of the ship. You were together on the Armada!"

Centuries later, I would return to Barcelona and hug the buildings, overwhelmed by a sensation of the city embracing me as her long-lost son!

On what would be our last ride through Griffith Park, I was given a horse named Bill. He was probably a retired breeding stallion, as he had an extra-wide girth. The groomsman adjusted the stirrups but I still couldn't get a grip around him. Gingi chided me saying I was making a big deal about nothing. I knew the horse was too big for me but I foolishly went along for the ride.

At the end of the morning, on our way back to the stables, the horses were hungry and began to run. Soon we were in full gallop across the prairie. Now when it was most important for my legs to have a good grip on the horse, I was bouncing up and down like a jack in the box.

Gingi rode up alongside me and screamed, "Hold on! Don't pull back on the reins!"

I knew that. I didn't need to be told. If I pulled back hard on the reins, I'd go flying right over the horse's head in a second. We were going at a pace of 25, maybe 30 miles an hour. It was all at once thrilling and terrifying. The wind whipped through my hair and the horse's mane. It was truly amazing that I was able to maintain balance without losing my grip or just slipping off the saddle.

When we finally arrived at the stables, I was relieved to see the groomsman come and take my horse by the reins as I gently slid off him, so grateful to have both my feet standing back on the ground. It was by far the most exciting ride ever.

Roni wandered off to smoke a cigarette and was sitting beneath a tree when I approached him gently. I could see that he was troubled and that I was partly the cause of those troubles.

I thought that if we continue like this, he might come to hate me and more importantly, I might hate myself. How could I walk through the world causing so much pain all the while claiming to know the truth? I had to tell him now that it was over between us, sexually speaking.

I was surprised at how hard he took it. I guess I thought he would be relieved, but he was not. He had fallen in love with me. He had given up his family in his heart and dreamed of being with me. I thought he was just making a bad joke when he said, "Just wait, you will pay for this, one day I am going to make you pay."

Years later standing in my stairwell he would warn me regarding a new lover of mine, "Don't take this guy from his family and then leave him. Believe me, it's not good."

I took it to heart, the grief I had not seen before. Our affair was the catalyst that had needlessly destroyed his marriage. They were probably meant for one another and lost each other then. I was convinced that Roni's primary interest had always been the draw of the heart. He was fascinated by the concept that there was something within him that was wonderful that he truly needed and could have, but he was full of fear. I would often go on about the amazing experience of peace within. The call to water for the thirsty is irresistible. We remained close friends of a somewhat dubious nature throughout the years.

Chapter Eleven — Cooper

Julie's Place was a splendid restaurant in the famous Pacific Design Center with a curved balconied staircase, a lovely dining room, and a cappuccino lounge. The uniforms were taupe or brown, floor length, off the shoulder, made of batiste jersey that clung beautifully. I asked the owner for a job. He took one look at me, and I was hired on the spot.

I was standing by the cappuccino machine at the entrance of the grand dining room looking quite statuesque, my long hair cascading over my shoulders. Suddenly I felt struck by an irresistible force that caused me to spin around. My eyes met the deep, penetrating glance of a man frozen in his tracks. We stood interlocked in a timeless space gazing at one another in awe. A brilliant tunnel of light could almost be seen flashing between us.

His friends stood staring until finally one of them nudged him on the shoulder, "Come on Coop."

He brushed him away with a wave and said, "Hey, wait a minute." And then he strode toward me, reaching out his hand, and introduced himself formally. "Cooper" was all I heard.

Later I would think he said "Jackie Cooper." That wasn't it. I was completely entranced. I didn't even ask myself who is this man. I didn't ask myself anything. I was taken with him from the moment we met. We both knew something extraordinary was about to happen.

He wasn't much taller than me and about the same weight. His clean-cut body was all tied up in a three-piece suit, with a Cartier watch strapped on, and wearing Fred Aster shoes. I actually didn't see any of that at the time. I only noticed the intense feeling of destiny that overwhelmed me. He would come back during lunch just to get my phone number privately.

I learned that he was the top salesman at Herman Miller, one of the largest design firms in the world. Many of their pieces still sit in Chicago Museum of Art. He was smart. He had style and class. He drove a Mercedes sedan around town while he left his 1957 Porsche Speedster in the garage untouched. Unlike most men with cars like that, he was the original owner. It was red with camel-colored leather interior. It was so clean you could have eaten off the engine, if he would ever let you near it. He routinely cleaned all the internal parts with a Q-tip, a regimen that made perfect sense for a man who served a term as president of the Porsche Club.

Bob Smith, a well-known car dealer, once asked him, "Do you ever take that Porsche out on the road?"

Cooper replied, "Only when they wash the streets with soap and water!"

The first time he called, I was housesitting at Joan Keller and Danny Selznick's place. Actually, it was Joan's home. Her father had commissioned an architect to design it for her as a graduation present. It was a beautiful home carved into the hillside just beneath the Hollywood sign. It had windows everywhere overlooking the surrounding woods.

The floors and outside deck were all terracotta, except the two bedrooms which had plush carpeting.

I had worked for Joan in the past, housekeeping twice a week. Now I just helped her with the occasional dinner party and stayed over when they were gone with the three Siamese cats and one standard poodle. I really liked Joan, and Danny was a sweet man, living under the shadow of his father, David O Selznick's enormous fame. Joan, on the other hand, was an extraordinary character in her own right. She was the first woman to win an Academy Award for a short subject documentary called *The Magic Machines*. She kept it with two of Danny's father's Oscars on the back of the toilet seat in the guest bathroom. Danny once said of her, "Eccentricity is its own reward."

Cooper called around 5:30 and after telling me very little about himself, asked if I would meet him for a drink. I set my hair, took a shower, put on some beautiful silk tap panties, slipped into one of Joan's Missoni dresses, and headed out the door. Copper was waiting for me in the Design Club, a private club for the designers at the PDC.

I was never much of a drinker and being that I was still macrobiotic I really didn't drink at all. So when Cooper asked what I would like to drink I ordered what was macrobiotically acceptable—a shot of Glenlivet in a snifter and a soda back. Since I've never really liked the taste of scotch, I would nurse that drink all night. The feelings of attraction for him that welled up within me were totally unexpected and a bit bewildering. I let myself be lulled into the charm of his presence.

A designer by education, he was a terrific salesman, and I was sold in our first glance. I wasn't looking for anyone, and my last thought would have been a corporate businessman, but he was very entertaining, amusing, witty, clever, and wise. He wore glasses sometimes and his face was so beautiful to me, despite the receding hairline. And he couldn't take his eyes off me as he asked questions about my life, intrigued by the answers. I guess I was far from anyone he would have been expecting as well.

Neither of us knew that this was the first of many nights we would spend together over the next four years. We would frequent all the best restaurants in town: The Palm, Trumps, Morton's, and even occasionally Julie's Place, where at night the dance floor became a discotheque and we would dance the night away. But now, in these first precious moments together, neither of us considered the future. Between us lay a great treasure that would change us both forever.

I don't remember if it was that first night or the second that he told me he was married. He had four children, the first of which was a girl adopted under unusual circumstances. How Cooper came in contact with the baby I don't recall, only that he took the infant home to his wife Anna and convinced her to accept an adoption. Next came two boys born of Anna. Then many years later, while they lived in Denver, he found another girl, twelve years old, the eldest of six, living in distressed conditions, and he successfully adopted her as well.

We wound up making out in his car that first night. He found my panties. "Oooh, you're a silk baby." His kisses as passionate as he was, I came in his hands.

Our next date was two nights later at one of Beverly Hills' finest restaurants, the Bistro Gardens. I was back in my own place now and made sure everything was in order before I left to meet him. Again, he was waiting for me, all suited up in a perfectly pressed shirt and tie, a true gentleman. He was 42 and I was 25. The fact that he was married seemed irrelevant to our relationship. The obstacles, the pain, and the anguish would show themselves later. I was convinced that he truly loved me and surrendered myself to him totally.

At the end of a sumptuous dinner served on white linen surrounded by bright green foliage, my wonderful new love followed me home to my bed. What an amazing lover he proved to be—so free, so full of burning passion. His body perfectly matched mine, and I loved the way our beautiful bodies were especially lovely together.

My girlfriend Marcie who lived next door once said, "When I hear you screaming in the night I just look outside my window, and if I see Cooper's car is there, I know you're alright!"

Cooper would go down on me until I was weeping and begging him to stop. We often made love through the night until dawn. Once he came six times in a night before leaving to go back to his wife. I felt pain when he left, even if it only meant an hour alone before the day began.

He cleverly brought me into the core of his family and defended me before his closest friends. I remember the first time he invited me to a family barbecue around the pool. His wife made a snide comment in front of me, something about Coop not being able to get it up. At least I had something she didn't.

Meanwhile, I was having powerful experiences in my practice of the gift of peace. I would sit for an hour or so before getting ready to come to work. I would start the morning in a state of bliss, but then the slightest thing could set me off. If you painted a wall white and someone put a black mark on it, what would you see? I guess the perfection within made the imperfections of the world more visible to me.

One of Cooper's colleagues approached me at work and ran his hand sensuously up and down my back. I spun around to confront him with such force that he began to run, and I ran after him. When I caught up with him, I pummeled his back with my fists. Neither he nor any of Cooper's associates would ever dare to take such liberty with me again. Cooper was amused.

Coop tried to convince me to join his world. He would say, "Hey you're gorgeous. You should be standing in a showroom." I couldn't picture myself as part of the business world at that time.

Cooper would gaze lovingly into my eyes and say, "Peace? I've already got peace. You should come to me for peace."

Then he'd grin, take another sip of his scotch on the rocks, usually White Label, and flip a cigarette into his mouth.

I only worked the lunch shift, usually serving drinks and the occasional meal. Cooper crossed through the bar area daily on his way to lunch with clients in the main dining room. Sometimes he would come over and acknowledge me, and sometimes he wouldn't. I usually figured it had something to do with that particular client, until he wandered in one day with his friends and walked by as if he didn't see me.

That afternoon I called my sister, Kate. After relating the story to her, she asked me if I knew how much he was drinking. I told her what I had seen him drink in the day. And then she told me that it sounded like mood swings to her and did I think there was a possibility that he was an alcoholic?

It had never occurred to me. I had never acknowledged that my father was an alcoholic and had carefully remained ignorant of what that actually meant. Kate suggested I read *I'll Quit Tomorrow* by Vernon Johnson.

I started to question Cooper about his drinking. Meanwhile, our lovemaking was better and better every time, a phenomenon that continued for years. We came together often. He was without question one of the best lovers of my life, if not the best, given the endurance and number of years. I was indelibly in love, as if I had loved him for centuries.

Cooper asked me if I would stay with his children over the upcoming four-day weekend. He and Anna would be going on a Porsche rally together, as they did every year. It made sense to me that Anna would go with him to something they had always done together. I did not feel threatened. I was surprised and honored that he wanted me to stay in his house and take care of his children, yet I agreed to his request apprehensively.

Cooper loved his children and he loved me. He wanted to bring me as close into his life as possible, and Anna was still none the wiser. How she thought that Cooper and I were just friends, that I was just a young woman he deeply respected and trusted, I don't know. Perhaps a wife will look away when she has too much to lose by facing it.

I was concerned how his children might behave towards me if they had any inkling that I was their father's lover, but I trusted Cooper's love for me. He wanted me to get to know his children and them to know me. He was sure they would love me too. I think if he had gone away with Anna and just left me alone, I might have been overwhelmed by jealousy. His request somehow made me feel cared for.

Each night when the children went to sleep, I practiced in Cooper's bedroom and slept comfortably in their bed. The beauty of the self, stirring within, took me far away from my concerns and doubt.

Cooper was an absolute perfectionist. A single fingerprint on the face of a designer clock would not do. His children were very well behaved, as the children of alcoholics often strive to be. They were kind, polite, and independent. Besides, they were terrified of his anger, an anger I would come to know later.

I became very close to his eldest and last adopted daughter. She was now a beautiful 14-year-old bright-eyed, smiling blonde named Jodi. She was interesting and intelligent. Her exuberance for life and the joy of it was a trait she shared with Cooper.

We spent most of our time together that weekend. I loved her as if she were my own child. And then the visions started rolling in. I had a vivid dream that Cooper and I were together on Atlantis. We were totally in love. Our beautiful blonde daughter was around Jodi's age. We lived in a gorgeous white Palazzo overlooking the sea, where many whitewashed houses were nestled against the hillside.

There was a tower-like monolith set on a small island just offshore. It was the power source, perhaps atomic. I don't know. I only know we all knew it was about to explode, and we had very little time left of our precious lives. We were planning to head for the island all together. For some reason everyone was gathering there. Perhaps we thought that since we could not avoid the oncoming destruction, we were going to merge with it somehow. Maybe we could let our spirits burn free?

In the dream, Cooper had a twin brother who desired me. The brother convinced me that my husband and daughter had already left without me and that he was supposed to take me to meet them. I trusted him. He took me across the water in a small rowboat to the island. But my husband had not left yet. He and my daughter were still waiting for me before leaving. His brother had deceived me in the hopes of satisfying his lust. I did not get the chance to kiss my family goodbye. We all died. In the morning I shared the dream with Jodi.

She commented, "I think the daughter was me."

Cooper and Anna returned home without incident to good reports all around. I began to daydream about the time when Cooper and I would live together. How would it be when he left Anna and married me? I wasn't born to be a kept woman. Though Cooper had offered to pay my measly $200 a month rent, I refused. But there was a bigger obstacle standing between us—his drinking.

It was Jodi who told me he started each morning with scotch on the rocks. I became concerned and read the book Kate had suggested cover to cover until I had thoroughly grasped it and understood Johnson's suggestion for forcing a surrender to treatment. He called it an intervention.

I was able to practice peace within, but Cooper was not able to drink himself to contentment. Nor was he even willing to consider an alternative to the floating anxiety his long-term addiction had trapped him in. The weight of his suffering began to fall on me. I could now feel his pain even when he made love to me, and I began to worry about him on his drive home, a little frantically at times. I had no way of knowing that he had gotten home safely until I spoke with him later that day.

An intervention involved gathering together his family and closest friends and confronting him by surprise in the morning before he could take his first drink. The purpose was to help an individual look into the mirror and see his troubled life with the sincere testimonies of his dearest ones reflecting the misery he was causing himself and them. It was expected that one would then break down with natural remorse and accept going into a treatment center.

I met with Jodi at a small restaurant near their home to tell her what I felt we needed to do and asked for her support. I realize now what a heavy burden that was to place on the shoulders of a teenager, though she was quite willing and eager to help, having herself witnessed his declining boundaries. She told me he once cornered her in the garage and tried to kiss her. He was drunk. She wiped her mouth as she recalled the appalling incident. We decided that she would tell Anna what we were up to when the time was right, as she would have to be in on it too.

I bided my time thinking every detail through as carefully as possible. I needed the help of his best friend at work as well, but trusting him was the critical variable that led to downfall.

Meanwhile, one night as Cooper lay in my arms, I had my hand resting above his liver when suddenly I noticed something strange. I saw three dark circles reflecting on the palm of my hand: one was the size of a quarter, one a nickel, and one a dime. I had never noticed such a phenomenon before. I knew I was able to radiate various colors of light from my hands, but I was not used to receiving shadows, colors, or images.

I said nothing to him about it that night but made up my mind to pay a visit to Dr. Tich Antangh. He was a Vietnamese M.D. from Paris University, a master of macrobiotics, martial arts, and was a Zen Buddhist priest! He had helped me recently when pain was pounding up the side of my neck and head. I was terrified it meant the return of the palsy. He suspected a stroke, but with the use of his herbs and strict adherence to the seventh regime of macrobiotics, I was completely healed within a few weeks.

So I went to ask him if the shadows I saw in my hand meant what I thought they meant. He said yes. It was the start of cirrhosis. Then he taught me a quick trick for diagnosing cancer. That was the beginning of my hands being able to read the body.

I decided to start treatment on him the next time he came over. As he rested in my arms after lovemaking, I laid my hand on his liver and began to radiate a cool green light. I was hoping to freeze the spotted area to stop it. He lay sleeping for the most part except for the three times when he woke complaining about how cold he was. I put a blanket over him, turned up the old gas heater, and then I realized it was working. All the blood goes through the liver, and it was chilling him.

It was time to meet with Anna. Jodi brought her to meet with me. Nothing was mentioned about my relationship with her husband. Either she did not know or did not care. I told her what she already knew, that Cooper was desperately and dangerously ill, that without our intervention now he could kill himself on the road at any time. I even suggested that it might be easier to just look the other way and let him die rather than try to help him. I explained what an intervention was and how we could go about it. She was extremely reluctant, scared, but she couldn't back away from the challenge I had placed before her. She agreed to help, picking the day it would be possible for us to all meet early in the morning in her home.

The night before, Anna phoned to call it off. Cooper found out, and he was furious with me. It cut him to the core. I had not only betrayed his trust, I had hurt his feelings and wounded him deeply.

I went looking for him. He was with his "real" friends, drinking at the Red Onion in Beverly Hills. He could hardly look at me. The more I protested my love and concern for him, the more he screamed at me, until finally, in a complete rage, he grabbed me by my shoulders, lifted me up off the barstool, and threw me against the wall. Then he insisted on taking me back to my car. We wound up in the parking lot of the Pacific Design Center. He dragged me out of his car by my hair. As soon as I raised my fist to him, it was over. He let go of me like a hot potato.

The next day the boss called me to his office up the grand staircase. He had heard about what happened the night before. He fired me. I figured Cooper had demanded it. The broken chance at an intervention wreaked havoc on his life and self-esteem. My heart was breaking, too, because I thought I had lost him forever. I would have stayed with him as a drunk rather than walk out of his life altogether.

Had I known the result would be this, would I have tried anyway? Yes, I certainly would have done anything and risked everything to help him. He closed himself behind his walls while he attempted to recover.

I told Kate what happened to our grand plan, and she was concerned about me. She asked me to see Milton

Erickson's colleague Ernest Rossi, to help with my recovery, as I had also been crushed by the whole experience. Rossi, like Erickson, was a specialist in hypnotherapy. However, I still could not be hypnotized, though I appreciated his kindness and understanding. I would not meet with him again until several decades passed.

Two weeks later Cooper remembered that he loved me and called, asking if I would join him for dinner. I was so happy and relieved. Of course, I ran to him. We never again discussed what had happened. But it had happened, and I began to view the possibility of a life with him differently. He announced at dinner that he was quitting smoking cigarettes, I figured to prove that he was capable of quitting something. He pointed out my addiction to cigarettes and occasionally chided me about it, as ex-smokers often do. We would still make love, but now I felt his pain, too.

Chapter Twelve — Jack

Within a few days of being fired from Julie's, I was hired at Tony Roma's in Beverly Hills, serving delicious ribs and coleslaw. Sherry, the manager, was a smart businesswoman and one of the best-dressed buxom women I have ever seen. She was also one of the most sought-after ladies in town, pursued by wealthy realtors, elite car dealers, and other bachelors who sought women of the highest class. I admired her. Unfortunately, the uniform was an embarrassment; it was a little brown fitted smock, cut short enough to see the ruffled panties underneath.

Lynn, the bookkeeper, sat in the small back office. Lynn was a six-foot tall, bawdy woman with a heroin problem. She liked me and got this idea that I should meet her other boss, an extremely prolific author named Jack. I told her I was involved with Cooper for a few years now. She insisted that Jack and I would get along, something about us both being smart and what a brilliant writer he was. I was intrigued.

"Okay, get me one of his books. I'll read it, and if I like it, I'll meet him."

The book she brought me was about a serial killer. I told Lynn I wasn't into blood and violence, but she persisted,

"Don't worry, all the gore is only shown through the eyes of the coroner."

I thought that was an interesting approach and took it home to read. Aside from the novel's excellent format and timing, I got the distinct impression that Jack was revealing an aspect of his own darkness. I found it to be courageous. When I finished reading it, I tried to hand it back to Lynn who said, "It's okay, he wants you to keep it."

As I complimented his work, a scream came through the bar. I dashed out and ran to help. There was a man who had fallen off a bar stool and was now writhing on the floor in a full epileptic fit.

I jumped down on my knees to help him, screaming over my shoulder, "Somebody get me a spoon! I need to pry his mouth open!" I had been taught that a spoon pressed against the tongue would effectively prevent someone from choking. I understand this method is no longer advisable, yet this treatment of spoon and tongue restraint was accepted in the 1970s, even if now it is discredited as an effective first aid for epilepsy.

I massaged his jaw, then jammed the spoon between his teeth and forced his mouth open. I knew I had to catch his tongue to keep him from swallowing it. Then I placed my hands on his chest and absorbed the shaking into my own body as my bewildered co-workers watched on.

As soon as he was at rest and fully conscious, I disappeared as was my custom, like how Superman escaped quickly after each rescue. I was reluctant to hang around and be thanked or praised for something of which I took no ownership. I had a skill that came as a result of my intense studies in Chi Gung. I was compelled to help those whom I could, whether or not I felt so inclined.

Lynn caught up with me after lunch and handed me Jack's number saying he was anxious to meet me and hoped I could drop by his condo that night. I showed up at his door in a darling cotton print dress. He was overwhelmed with attraction from the moment he opened the door. I felt his kind and gentle nature right away when he beckoned me to come in, reaching out his hand to welcome me. "Thank you for coming. Lynn has told me so much about you, though she did not aptly describe your beauty."

I smiled, appreciating his obvious though charming come on. He was a tall man of some girth with well-bred manners and a certain elegance about him. But it was his extreme intelligence that I was most attracted to. Supposedly his cumulative IQ was 190, whatever that means.

His place was on La Cienega, just south of Sunset, on the first floor facing the front with a view of the city. It was the classic one-bedroom bachelor pad, well designed with modern leather chairs, a comfortable sectional, and a glass coffee table. The walls were decorated with impressive works of art. He offered me a drink and then walked me over to the bookcase, where he pointed out his several published books, before we sat down across from one another.

He began to interview me, asking questions about my history, my current circumstances, and hopes for the future. Jack filled me in on his credentials as well. He took his undergraduate degree from SMU and a Master's from Harvard. His first writing job was with The New York Times, as a cub crime reporter, in the homicide division. Most recently he had published the first women's health encyclopedia with a famous doctor, which was translated into 36 languages.

Beginning to feel quite comfortable, Jack got up and strolled casually into the kitchen. I followed just far enough to lean over the bar that sectioned off the dining room. He hesitated for a second or so, staring at me as if making an appraisal, all the while keeping his hand on the knob of a small drawer.

Then he asked, "Have you ever tried cocaine?"

"Never," I replied. "Do I want to?"

"Well, I find it helpful for concentration while writing and sometimes I use it for recreational purposes. I have some if you'd like to try it."

"Sure," I said without a second thought.

Years ago, before receiving the gift, I would never have considered taking a narcotic of any sort. I had the least experience with psychedelics of anyone I knew. But now that I had the gift, I thought I was invincible. I feared nothing and was willing to try anything once. So as this gentle man was offering me a taste of something new, why wouldn't I?

Jack pulled open the drawer and lifted out a glass mirror, on which were several lines of some white powder. He took a $100 bill, rolled it up like a straw, and showed me how to snort it. I took two hits. Wow, what a rush! Instantly I became so clearheaded, so bright, surely whatever I said was going to be pure genius. Definitely it took the conversation up several notches.

Now Jack revealed his deepest sorrows and fears to me. His unwed mother had given him up to an orphanage when he was an infant. He stayed there until he was finally adopted at age 4. A lawyer and his wealthy wife, who became his parents, changed his name entirely when they signed the papers. And now, for some inexplicable reason, he was afraid he would never write again. I quickly assured him that I knew he would. I wasn't sure how I knew that, but I would soon find that the cocaine bumped up my psychic abilities to a point that would one day soon become unbearable for me.

As the night lingered on, Jack would eventually discover that I had a lover and that we had been together for several years. But that news did not dissuade him. He was bound and determined to have me one day come hell or high water. When it was time for me to leave, we embraced. Then he looked me in the eyes and asked if he could kiss me. That was his first mistake, he asked. He received a cursory peck on the lips, and I was out the door after agreeing to have dinner with him the next night.

Jack picked me up from my home the next evening in his Lancia with license plates that said "Author." He took me to the Bistro Gardens, the same place Cooper and I had gone on our first date, not that this was a date.

We had a fabulous dinner, and he was a perfect gentleman. When the meal was finished, the waiter brought the check to me. It wasn't the first time that happened, and it wouldn't be the last. Apparently, I have a commanding nature at the table that sometimes leads the waiter to believe I am in charge. Jack, of course, quickly grabbed the check and paid it. He asked if I'd like to stop by his place for a bit on the way home.

"Sure," I said.

Out came the cocaine plate, and we were off and running. Now he confessed that he was in fact selling cocaine in large quantities and calling it "The Material". A page was a gram, a chapter was an ounce, and a book was a kilo. Of course, he was just doing it for a little extra money on the side.

As he drew a few more lines for us to snort he cautioned, "Be careful, this isn't candy, it can creep up on you."

This was fun, I thought. Interesting. Exhilarating.

I didn't have more until a few weeks later when we went out again, this time to a restaurant called "La Masia". Jack handed me a small white packet when I arrived, almost the moment I sat down at the table, telling me I could go and take a hit in the bathroom.

I went into a stall, locked the door, opened the packet, and just before I took a hit, the thought crossed my mind, "Is he making me addicted to this?" Just as quickly I dismissed such a thought. No one could make me anything. If I were to become addicted, it would be my responsibility, my fault, and mine alone. I would continue to maintain that stance despite the disasters that were about to befall me.

Jack had asked me to work for him as his assistant on a part-time basis to begin with. He was in full pursuit of me, and he wanted to have me around him at any cost. I would be running his errands, straightening up, and occasionally going to the library to research. He persisted in asking for more, but when I told him that I was committed to Cooper, he said he wanted me in his life no matter what.

More and more we went out together socially. Jack was extremely entertaining. He was well versed in seemingly every possible subject, and his expertise in trivia was unmatched. He did, however, have a propensity for telling both racist and anti-Semitic jokes.

One night before a party I told him, "You tell one more of those jokes, and this will be the last party I go to with you." He took me seriously, promised not to, and kept his word. He was on the A-list for Hollywood parties. The fact that he supplied cocaine might've had something to do with it. We were entertained in the homes of the top actors, directors, and producers of the time.

One of those parties was at the home of Severn Darden. Severn was a comedian, an actor and a founding member of *The Second City*, a Chicago based comedy troupe. He received a Tony nomination for his performance in their Broadway musical revue, *From the Second City*. He was among the many Jack counted as friends. When we arrived, we were ushered into a bedroom where a woman was displaying her newly framed black-and-white photography.

As we gazed over her work Jack asked which one would I choose to keep. Of course, my choice was his as well. We went on to the dining room, where twelve guests were seating themselves around a large oval bouquet table. Just as I sat down Severn called out to me saying, "Would you come here for a minute?"

I got up and walked over to him. He had never met me before that evening, which made his next request all the more concerning.

"Would you please just place your hands on my chest for a moment?"

I stood behind his chair and placed my palms on his heart, as the stunned guests looked on. I closed my eyes to let my hands see. His heart needed to heal.

I let my healing energy pour through him for several moments and then silently returned to my place at the table. Many, many years later he would die from congestive heart failure, but this night he could breathe easy. It was the first time I was called out by a complete stranger, intuitively knowing I could help him, but this would be repeated with increasing frequency throughout my life. As we left, Severn presented me with a beautiful peach-colored, cowl neck cashmere sweater, which I accepted graciously and wore for years until it turned to rags.

It was the '80s, and cocaine was everywhere, even factored into the budget of films. I thought I had it under control. I casually suggested that my girlfriend Patty might like to try it as well. So Jack gave me two small white envelopes of a gram each and told me I could take it to her. I would like to think it was before I realized it could be dangerous that I took that first gram to Patty.

It was late afternoon when I stopped by her small West Hollywood home and handed her one of the tiny packages smiling. "Here, try this with Eli."

"Okay," she said in her cute southern way. We smoked pot together regularly, so I figured she might like this too. I didn't stay long because I was on my way to Roni's shop with the other packet. When I arrived at the shop and handed it to Roni, telling him what it was, he looked at me quite sternly and said, "What are you doing with this? This is not for you."

Little did I realize that the Israeli mafia was neck deep into cocaine. But I would soon find out. One night, Roni called me to come down to the shop saying he had something he wanted to show me. It was pretty late at night but I went down anyway. He told me to come around to the back door when I arrived. There I would find him sitting in the narrow back storage room with a glass pipe and some things that looked like little white rocks. I guess, as he knew I was now snorting coke, he felt free to bring me in on this as well. As usual, I would try almost anything once.

"Sit down," he said.

Next thing I knew he was putting a glass pipe in my mouth and lighting the rock cocaine inside the bowl with a small torch. "Take a hit," he said.

He was obviously excited just watching me draw on it. I held it in for a moment and then blew it out. The sensation was overwhelmingly powerful. It was a weird kind of ecstasy that filled every pore of the body. I believe I was hooked from the first hit. We stayed there smoking it in that tiny room until dawn. I knew it was wrong for me to be there, to be smoking with him, because it encouraged him to think it was okay. The downward spiral started to become very slippery. I didn't tell Jack about it at first, but when I did, he said he found it disgusting and that he would never do it.

I never discussed it or shared it with Cooper. I still thought I could hold it together with him. But Jack was becoming more and more amorous, and finally one night I gave in. He was passionate and intent on pleasing me. He gave excellent head and wanted it in return. Unfortunately, he enjoyed the sound of me gagging, and that was a huge sexual turnoff for me. I eventually got up and said, "No, I cannot do this. I am with Cooper."

"Okay, I understand, it won't happen again." But of course, it did, again and again. Now my life was full of money and cocaine. Jack stored loads of cash all around the house and showed me every hiding place. He trusted me implicitly. He regarded me as a spiritual person who could do no wrong.

I wrote a short essay on the subject of his product and called it:

"The Material"

Conclusions on cocaine

The obvious addictive reaction is up down. The rush is at best a fleeting excitement, venerable yet invincible. Years before I ever saw the stuff, a young stranger described the high to me saying, "You feel like you are the Prince of the Universe." Interesting the accuracy of that image, the arrogance that leads into hours of conversation over imagined brilliance, passing the glass, reaching for a straw whenever doubt by the downslide begins to creep in. It's insidious, the sad fakery we engage in, in order to forestall the fear that builds with wanting each new line.

You live, you work, you start to make money, and the pressure to be the cleverest, the shrewdest, builds to desperate proportions. You buy in, you believe you are good, you are loving. Blown away, you dream of the ghosts you love, making plans, staying on top of it all at any cost. After all, everyone does it, so why not? How else can I compete and win? But the "how else" is soon forgotten, the seduction is too powerful, it carries you to a place that pretends to be safe and then drops you into the longing for another taste, the sensual draw up into the head, the apparent clearing that numbs the senses and suffocates the heart.

Under this "truth serum" the emotions are erased. Racing by reality with confidence, ignoring the inevitable crash, we pat each other's backs, "It's cool, we're cool," take the edge off, have a drink. Escape the confronting trip down, drop a "lude." No problem, go into the bathroom, draw against the walls, hiding until from somewhere within, the creeping sensation of a stirring aloneness calls you from somewhere unknown. Suppress the aching, numb yourself, do more. You know you are addicted when you suspect it, but you can't admit it, and considering the possibility evokes a pain not easily pushed back.

I showed it to Jack. He was impressed. I think it was the first time I'd showed him a sample of my writing besides the poetry, and this began a discussion of my possibilities as a writer rather than a realistic examination of the content and its meaning for us. I was sinking deeper and deeper into oblivion, and I didn't realize it.

My new drug interest was overriding my need for Cooper's love. I had been able to keep them separate. But my use, though always intermittent, greatly influenced the days in between. And now, once I took that first hit, I wanted it all night. When there was no more left, I would go to extraordinary lengths to get more. The psychological and emotional pain coming down was so intense, I ached for it in my bones.

We would drink to try and come down faster when we knew we could not get more that night, which often had become morning. I would drive home in agony. There was no way I wanted to lay next to anyone in that condition. I never understood how some people felt sexual on it. I'd stop at a 7-Eleven for Nytol and take as much as I dared.

Once home I prayed to God to help me sleep and let me wake to a new day. I clung to whatever thread of my internal experience of peace I was able to grasp and used it as an anchor to hold still while I counted my breaths. I started to avoid Jack. Meanwhile, almost everyone I knew was doing it. Invitations to join in were often, and this was only the beginning.

The first time I stole was from Jack. I had been getting high all night and into the next day. When it was gone, and the pain began to set in, I was desperate to get more. I knew Jack's housekeeper would have been there in the morning, and that Jack had meetings in town all day. Since I had a key to his place and knew where the money was, I went and took a handful from between the towels in the linen closet. I rationalized that money earned from drug dealing was ill-gotten gains anyway.

I had never stolen so much as a piece of gum and was now a thief. A few days would go by before Jack and I were sitting across from each other in his living room again. He gently and kindly gave me the opportunity to confess, but I could not. He didn't directly accuse me. He just mentioned that there was money missing, and I acted as if I knew nothing about it. He knew, and I knew he knew, but he let it go, though he eventually took his key back.

I was quietly grateful and he didn't say another word. He did ask if I would run an errand for him, explaining that he was not able to do it himself this time. He wanted me to take a kilo to his partner Max in Upland. He apologized for asking me to take such a risk and promised it would be the one and only time. After he explained that everything would be well secured so there should be no problem, I agreed to do it because I thought I owed him something.

It was a long drive out there, over an hour. I was counting the minutes to arrival. Finally reaching my destination, I was greeted at the door by Max, a big burly guy with a warm and welcoming nature. I was beginning to notice a code of ethics among criminals. I was definitely entering the gangster world and was almost amused by how friendly they all appeared to be on the surface at least. After examining the contents of the package I'd delivered, he asked if I'd like to take an eighth back to Jack. I agreed. It was properly packaged and with a quick hug goodbye I was led out the front door and back into Jack's car.

There were always enough days between episodes that I still appeared to be leading a normal life. I was careful not to accept invitations to get high on a night before a workday. Problems began to occur when I continued on for 24 hours, and then it would go for 48 hours. But so far, I thought I had my addiction under control. I was a weekender.

One late night I received a call from Patty asking if I'd like to come over and sit with Eli and her. I started to notice that I was much more likely to say yes when I was ovulating or about to start my period. So this time I said, "Sure." And off I went.

When I arrived at their new condo near the art museum, I found Eli sitting on the couch lining up a plate full of cocaine. Patty was more stoned than I'd ever seen her, sitting on the floor adjacent to Eli, her legs wide open commando style, her hairy black mound out for all to see. I was startled, to say the least! She had never come onto me before, and I wasn't really sure she was now. I had the feeling Eli put her up to it. I knew their relationship, and it was she who primarily called the shots. I was embarrassed even to look at her, and whatever it was they were expecting of me, I had no intention of giving a performance for Eli. I never regretted that decision. I knew our friendship could not survive it. I left.

The cocaine high occasionally reminded me of what I really loved, the gift. I would find myself trying to convince those I sat snorting with of its miraculous value. How could me getting high with them be a testament to its Truth? I was sought after as safe company for those who chose to lock themselves away over a table full of white powder and they poured their hearts out to me.

It was late one morning after smoking with Roni all night long that I dropped by Jack's place not really expecting him to be there. I probably knew he had a lunch appointment with the manager of a famous country rock singer-songwriter whose biography they had approached him to write.

I parked my car in the underground lot, went up the elevator, and knocked on his front door just to see if he was there. He didn't answer, so I figured he had already gone, and I went to the pool area where there was a wall I could jump over to get to the condo next to Jack's and then jump over the patio wall to get to his place. So I did, and to my great relief, the sliding door had been left open.

Once in the condo I went straight for the kitchen drawer and found on the mirror a large pile of cocaine. I grabbed a sheet of typing paper, made an envelope, and took half of it with me. Then I left through the front door.

The next time I tried that trick it turned out he was actually there sleeping in his bedroom. He woke up and caught me just as I was breaking the lock on the door. He shook his head with a look of exasperation, disgust, and anger, perhaps mixed with the thought, "Well, actually I brought her here." He shook his head and let me out the front door, with not so much as a word.

I was mortified and could say nothing either. The physical as well as mental agony of needing the drug was so unbearable. I had so often judged addicts; now I had surely become one. Oh, maybe I was just a weekender but that was enough to get me lost. Now I had given him the chance to think he was better than me, and he would use it against me. His ammunition was gossiping. Did he hate me, himself, or what we had both become?

As brutally as the reality of all this fell upon me, I knew it was a sickening illusion from which I would one day recover. I found infinite forgiveness within myself, yet the battle with my demons raged on. My studies had trained me to be capable of extraordinary things. Knowing what to surrender and what to set aside would take time.

That morning I took the envelope home with me and snorted most of it by myself. Luckily, I never learned to cook it! Jack thought the rock manager had taken the stuff when he turned his back, and it blew the entire deal out of the water! I never confessed that it was me who took the load off the plate. Stupidly I bottled some of it and took it with me to a musical we attended that night. There always comes a point after hours and hours of doing cocaine where the feeling is just so sickening and no other hit is going to make it any better, yet you try on and on until it is gone and you just cannot get anymore. Then perhaps you crawl around on a motel carpet floor, searching for a tiny piece of rock that might have dropped. Thankfully, in my home, the floors were wood.

Meanwhile, I was offered the lunch manager position at a new restaurant on La Cienega called "Rockwell's", having been recommended by Sherry, my manager at Tony Roma's. I accepted the job because it was a break from waitressing and an interesting new challenge. The restaurant was beautiful; the chef was excellent but difficult. In the midst of a busy lunch one day, he fired one of my waiters. It was the first time I learned that a chef had the power to do that. If he refused to make the waiter's orders, there was nothing I could do about it. I had to let him go.

In an effort to create more business for our Sunday brunch, I hired a jazz band headed by Joseph, a gorgeous, young black man and one of the finest jazz musicians I would ever know. His hands were beautiful, and his music was amazing. When he played, I got hot and wet. I wanted him, and as it turned out, he wanted me as well; another secret lover hidden from Cooper. I loved the contrasting colors of our skin, the rich black against my pale white. And the sex was good because I cared for him deeply. I believe he fell in love with me, but I backed off from a serious sustained relationship with him for so many reasons, though we've remained lifelong friends.

Jack was still in love with me, or so he thought. He wanted me, he desired me, and he enjoyed my company, as I did his. But I could not return the love he had for me. I loved him very dearly, but not romantically. Though we were seen together all over town and thought by many to be a couple, I was still in love with Cooper, and Jack knew it.

And there would be others along the way. How I kept everyone separate, with none of my many worlds and relationships colliding, is amazing to me now. There would come a time when Jack's love and admiration turned to resentment. But whatever was between Jack and I, we would remain in one another's lives. Our relationship would survive the test of time, though unthinkable trials, desperate years, and brutal betrayals. Until one day a bright light would drop between us, and its warmth would bind us together forever.

Chapter Thirteen – Steiger

Rod Steiger invited Jack to a barbecue at his home in the Malibu Colony one lovely early summer day. Rod and he had recently met and were interested in developing their friendship. Rod had told Jack he could bring a friend and I was the lucky one. Jack had told me in confidence that Rod just had quadruple bypass surgery. Rod didn't want anyone in the industry to know, because it would be the death knell to his career. The cost of insuring Steiger on a film set after such a surgery would have been phenomenal.

We arrived early in the afternoon. Rod proudly told Jack that he had played tennis that morning for the first time in six months. I knew very little about Rod before meeting him. I had only seen a few of his films like *Dr. Zhivago, In the Heat of the Night*, and *Oklahoma* filmed for TV in black-and-white. His greatness as an actor was in all the characters he created, unique, original, and nothing at all like him.

The small guest list included, writer/producer Phillip Rosenberg, director Norman Jewison, whose wonderful Moonstruck would years later warm my romantic heart, and the actor Michael Douglas with his first wife.

Rod's quaint beach house in Malibu Colony was comprised of three structures: the main house, the brightly windowed studio/office, and a small guesthouse with a pool. In the main house, the brick fireplace was adorned with a glittering array of awards including an Oscar, a Golden Globe, two BAFTAs and the New York Film Critic's Circle award. On the walls hung paintings from some of my favorite artists such as Cezanne, Picasso, and my very favorite, Van Gogh.

I went out onto the back lawn that bordered his private beach and stood on a wooden step above the sand exclaiming aloud to the sky, "God, what a beautiful day!"

"You're welcome!" retorted Rod, who was suddenly standing right behind me. I turned around and smiled.

"Thank you for allowing me to come."

"Oh! You are most welcome." He grinned, eyes glistening and went back in to check on the chicken wings he was marinating.

I wandered into the living room to examine the art. Just then my eyes fell upon a small framed etching. It was one of Van Gogh's sketches of his doctor. I sat down beside it to get a closer look.

"Touch it and an alarm goes off." Rod whispered in my ear.

I smiled again. We spent a moment discussing our love of Van Gogh. I was attracted to him, and he was clearly attracted to me. Impassioned souls always recognize each other.

He was out grilling chicken on the barbecue when I sidled up to him and he asked, "Are you Jack's girlfriend?"

"No, I work for him."

Without looking at me and turning chicken all the while he said, "Tell me your number. Just say it, I'll remember."

I did. Then we carried the food to the picnic table in the yard overlooking the sand and the sea. Rod made excellent teriyaki chicken. Everyone was happy, friendly, and it turned out to be a boisterous barbecue.

**

I hadn't started working in the film industry yet though Jack was pushing me to get an agent. He had even arranged for a photographer to help build my portfolio. We finally found a kindly old gentleman just down the street from him who was willing to take me on. The agent gave me a long list of casting agents and advised me to send my headshots out to every one of them. I looked at the names and thought, *He must be kidding me, who are these people?* Turns out they were the top casting directors in town, and I still see their names in film credits.

**

We all gathered in Rod's living room, lingering a little longer.

Michael Douglas asked Rod, "If your house was burning down, and you could only save one, which of these paintings would you take?" Without hesitation, Rod pointed to the one behind my head. It was the Van Gogh sketch I had been admiring earlier.

I didn't mention to Jack that I'd given Rod my phone number. Two days later Rod called and asked if I would like to come down to Malibu for dinner. I said yes, of course. We were going to La Scalia for our first date.

I arrived at his home to find him underdressed and wearing a white cap with a hole in it. It was his disguise. He did not like being recognized in public. We laughed all the way to the restaurant, and after a bottle of wine, we would sing all the way home.

Rod was so much like me. I loved being with him and he could not take his eyes off me. The chef himself came out to take our order. It was delightful having dinner with him; his conversation was exciting and witty. He was so full of life and history, and when I spoke, he hung on my every word. Unfortunately, he had already heard about the Teacher from a slightly wacky Englishwoman, who was his housekeeper for a while. It's hard to break first impressions, and besides, Rod liked to see himself standing with the gods on Mt. Olympus, in need of nothing from anyone.

I didn't realize how quickly he was falling in love with me. He said he wanted to work with me as an actress. He was serious. When we got back to his home that night, he poured me a glass of Napoleon Brandy.

I went up to his bedroom with him. He undressed me. I really wanted to make love to him, though the hanging flesh of a much older body was a bit of a turnoff, but his amazing passion and desire to please made me hot and wet. I wanted him and I was comfortable with him. I guess in some way I did love him within the limitation that I could love myself.

In the morning as I was leaving, Rod asked how soon I'd be back. I just smiled, kissed him, and said, "Call me."

Meanwhile, Cooper and I were still dating regularly. He knew very little about Jack except that I was occasionally working for him. And he knew absolutely nothing about Steiger. I had long ago stopped dreaming that we would ever be together as husband and wife but still, he was who he was to me, who he is, who he will always be.

So when he asked me to go away with him to San Francisco on a two-day business trip, of course I said yes. We stayed at the Embarcadero, and after his meetings we went to Scoma's for dinner.

He had this gentle, slightly aggressive way of lecturing me. I suppose he was trying to teach me something about myself that I still could not hear or listen to. "You're wasting your life! You should be teaching people what you know. You're fucking brilliant!"

I glared at him, ripped off a crusty piece of bread and threw the rest down on the plate, whereupon it skipped off and landed on someone else's entrée three tables away. Cooper was furious. Out of love and respect he was trying to tell me something. Today I know why and wonder, did he know what I was up to?

Meanwhile, I was still able to walk from one world to the other unhindered. Roni continued calling me on occasion to the back-alley entrance where we would sit in that tiny room that tested the limits of my claustrophobia and smoke all night long. He would profess his love and desire for me, and I would insist on speaking about the gift. It was all I could think about when I was high and Roni enjoyed hearing about it. After all, what better subject could be discussed in the maniacal conversations that would otherwise take place? I knew that I could not continue to sit with him like this. He and Ronite had separated, and he was living alone now. I decided to find him a girlfriend who also practiced the gift.

Marin was a curly-haired blonde of irresistible beauty. I first saw her sparkling energy dancing through the aisles of Larchmont Hall. She had the most beautiful smile and was as warm and friendly as anyone could possibly be. Her kindness was matched only by her generosity. She and I soon became friends.

I loved her.

Her father was Marion Parsonnet, who wrote the screenplay for Gilda, Rita Hayworth's signature role. Sadly he was to die at the tragically early age of 55. Her mother remarried shortly thereafter.

Marin had married an Italian screenwriter who had one major success which in this business could be enough to live on for a long time. They had a home in Valley Village. He loved her and was devoted to her like the Virgin Mary, except in bed where he treated her like a whore, she confided.

When I told Roni about Marin, he asked to meet her. As she also liked coke, she agreed. We all ended up smoking together that night. Marin had never smoked cocaine before and she was quite taken by the enhanced high, as well as by him.

They were wildly, fatally attracted to one another, so much so that when I was ready to leave, Marin stayed, and that was the beginning. I was relieved to have the responsibility of watching over Roni off me, but I quickly became more deeply concerned with Marin's plight. She was married and seeing Roni on the side. For his part, Roni fell desperately in love with her and would remain so the rest of his life. He would do anything to keep her with him and was intensely jealous of every breath she took when she was away from him.

They called me to join them on a regular basis, sometimes as a referee, sometimes as entertainment, sometimes as a paramour. If they were tired of my presence or just suddenly wanted to be alone to have sex, they would ask me to go out of the room for a few moments. The moments turned into hours. I would wait and wait hoping to be let back in, all the while aching for the drug that took out its wrath upon me. Repeatedly, I would go back to the door, knocking and knocking asking to come in, and then begging.

The same scene would take place over and over again, to worsening degrees. I remember once standing in the hallway of a motel on Sunset across from the famous Intercontinental. I was totally destroyed, unable to drive, begging for them to let me back in and pleading to God to let me remember this moment. I thought if I could remember I wouldn't wind up there again. Oh, but I would. They would let me back in for just a little bit, and then I would gather myself up and find the courage to drive home, swearing I would never let myself get there again.

Rod knew nothing of my intermittent drug life. I became an expert at hiding my deleterious activities, secretly playing so many different roles. Rod seriously wanted to work with me, but I did not want to use him to gain work. How foolish was I?

One day I went to his home and found him sitting in the living room absolutely still, as if paralyzed, staring off into the distance over the sea. He didn't speak at all, even as I stood there regarding him in the silence. It was the day before he was to start work on The Chosen, playing the role of the Hasidic Rabbi.

"Rod, what's wrong?" I said.

"I don't think I can do it," he said it a low undertone.

"Do what?" I asked.

"Act," he replied.

When they shot a scene in the streets of Brooklyn, where he danced with a tribe of the Hasidim, no one realized he was not really a rabbi! Rod was the consummate actor, without doubt one of the greatest that ever lived. But this powerful artist grappled with his own insecurity. He was a human being just like everyone else and he knew it.

When I reminded him that Laurence Olivier heaved backstage before every performance, he brightened up a bit, and we decided to go out for dinner.

Upstairs in his beautiful bedroom with its open beam ceilings and that comfortable bed, he held me by my shoulders for a moment looking deeply into my eyes and asked, "Will you wait while I shave? These days it's a delicate matter!"

"Sure."

He went into the bathroom, and I wandered out onto the balcony. There was a trellis that I could climb up to the roof, so I did. When Rod came out of the bathroom I was nowhere to be found. He called for me, and I did not answer. I let him wander back downstairs through the house calling my name and still, I did not answer. Only when he made it all the way out to the beach did I stand up on the roof and call to him, waving. He was totally surprised and amused. I ran down and wrapped him in a wild embrace. We truly had fun together!

The next day Rod called to say, "They've asked your old man to be the MC at the Simon Wiesenthal Institute's Humanitarian Award dinner for Elizabeth Taylor. It's a big deal: Century Plaza Hotel, big stars, lots of money. Will you come with me?"

Steiger was of Bavarian German descent and raised a Lutheran, not a Jew, but had strong ties to Israel. I never asked about that. I think there are lines in friendship, unspoken borders that you just don't question; you know the edge is there.

Whatever made Steiger a defender of Jews, I never knew. It was one more admirable quality of his, showing the depth of his humanity and he did receive an Oscar nomination for his role as a Jew in *The Pawnbroker*.

How deep was the respect of the Jewish community that Rabbi Hier would ask Rod Steiger to be the Master of Ceremonies for this event! Elizabeth Taylor had just finished narrating the Wiesenthal Institute's documentary with Orson Welles.

Would I go with him? Of course, I would be delighted! I did not yet know that my hero Simon Wiesenthal himself would be there! We decided it was best for me to meet him there, as Century City is in the middle of Hollywood and Malibu. The event was less than a week away. He must've affirmed his trust in me the night before, making him feel comfortable to invite me at nearly the last moment.

The perfect dress was hanging in my closet, a gift from Suzy Cream Cheese that she had never worn. It was a tailored black rayon knit with deep cut white satin lapels and cuffs. The flared skirt fell to the ground and moved gracefully in my long strides. I wore it with a white, black, and gray striped satin belt, tied neatly around my waist. Tall and elegantly thin, my statuesque figure fit the dress perfectly. It was as if it had been hanging in my closet just waiting to be worn that night.

A neighbor suggested that it needed a large piece of jewelry to fill the plunging neckline, offering to loan me a golden medallion on which "Allah" was inscribed in Arabic. The inscription was faint enough to render it unreadable from any distance, and any idea of impropriety never even occurred to me.

Rod was quite pleased to see me when I arrived, proud as he stood there in his tux, gazing at his beautiful girl. I remember feeling especially close to him that night. For him, it was us against them. He was often uncomfortable in the Hollywood crowd, a sensitive man, perhaps a bit too easily slighted. There was the long-standing conflict between him and Marlon Brando. I know that Rod respected Brando as an actor, but there was some bad blood over *On the Waterfront*. I don't remember what exactly.

We stood together at the end of the room for a while watching the guests file in. As women entered in beaded gowns, Rod said, "Here comes money."

Suddenly up walked ABC News. Lights, camera, action, and then surprisingly the mike was turned to me, as Rod stood by my side. They asked me, not Rod, what I thought of Elizabeth Taylor. I could almost hear Rod holding his breath, as he knew me to be a harsh critic of actors.

"Not only is Elizabeth Taylor one of our finest actresses but she's also one of the most beautiful women in the world!"

Rod literally wiped the sweat off his brow. He was so grateful. I may not always behave but at least I know how.

Then entering through a side door, proceeded by his security, was the impressive figure of the great Simon Wiesenthal. I actually bowed to him, as a show of my deep respect, admiration, and gratitude. He was known as The Nazi Hunter, devoting his life to hunting down the atrocious murderers from the SS. For the first and only time in my life, I was truly star-struck.

Eventually, those of us at the dais table would be ushered to the backstage area. It was there that I had the great pleasure of meeting Natalie Wood. She was so friendly, open, and genuine, utterly unencumbered by the fame game. Perhaps it was because she made her first film when she was six years old that the industry was home to her.

Rod introduced me to the amazingly soft-spoken, gracious lady herself, Elizabeth Taylor. Her light whispery voice was shocking to me after so many memories of her harsh, thundering performances in Virginia Woolf and The Taming of the Shrew.

Eventually, we were led out to the dais tables row by row. Rod and I were in the front, just to the right of the podium. Sammy Davis, Jr. and his wife were to my right. Elizabeth Taylor, Senator Warner, Simon Wiesenthal, and Rabbi Hier were seated in that order from the left of the podium. On the floor beneath us were 1,500 of the industry's most important players, stars and major donors of the Institute. No one had any idea who I was, but there I sat onstage with the biggest names in Hollywood, the rest of that world at our feet. I was an unknown interloper playing my role to perfection.

A sumptuous dinner was served amidst the cheerful revelry of the guests, so glad to be at this wonderful star-studded event. Once dessert and coffee had been served, it was time to preview the center's first documentary film called Genocide: The Story of the Holocaust.

Elizabeth had given her time and talent to narrating the film and had also brought Orson Welles in on the project. I was completely shaken by the horrible visions that I could not look away from now. Unaware of all but the pitiful scenes on the screen, I was overcome with hatred for the Nazis, and at one point, unconscious of all else, I shook my fist at the Nazis in front of everyone.

Rod would hear about that later. And he would defend me saying, "That's her. Her emotions run deep and bubble to the surface." Then it was time for Elizabeth to be presented her award. She accepted it with such humility and spoke from the depth of her humanity, in her ever-so-soft voice. She told how difficult it was for her to watch the pain and suffering, yet how important it was for the generations going forward to remember this time, "*when death became so ordinary, when torture was so trite, silence so pronounced.*" She showed herself, in her clear compassion, to be most worthy of her award. I was overwhelmed by the honor I felt just being there that night. The film would go on to win the Oscar for Best Documentary Feature in 1982.

Both the stage and floor audience lingered on long after the event concluded. As my hero was only a few chairs away, I took the chance and walked over to thank Simon Wiesenthal for his great work. He responded by letting me sit on his lap and giving me a warm, firm hug. What a sweetie!

When Rod and I were leaving that night, the paparazzi were still lurking. Rod agreed reluctantly that it was probably safer for me to go home from there, rather than try to follow him back to Malibu, considering how much we had both been drinking. Not that either of us were drunk. So he walked me back down to my car in the parking lot, kissed me, and thanked me for coming and behaving in a manner that had made him very proud. I hopped in my car and drove directly to Jack's, where I would end the night snorting cocaine with him.

A photograph of Rod and me wound up in the National Enquirer the next day with this note: "Veteran actor Rod Steiger stepping out in tinsel town with the dark-haired actress... They were together at a special tribute dinner for Liz Taylor the other evening, and Steiger admitted he and the beautiful 'woman' are regular date mates."

Though this would have delighted any other actress in town, it was a problem for me, because Cooper would now know immediately. And though he would never even refer to it, I realized I needed to make a choice.

The next time I went to Rod's I was greeted by his dear friend Dirk, who told me that Rod's comment about our picture showing up in the Enquirer was, "It can't hurt the kid."

Rod was sitting by the dining room table when I entered, musing on the death of Henry Miller, that had occurred six months earlier. He'd penned a poem, which he gave me to read. I thought it was inspired and told him so. He took a piece of his personal stationery and wrote the poem down to give me, saying, "Now you can't say I never gave you anything." It read:

he's dead
that big phallic kid
in his sleep!
god, how lucky
wonder what he knew
he must have known something
to go like that
at home
88
now that's it

all in one crystal ball
tropic
cancer
and
the clown at the foot of the ladder
smiling

That night at dinner, Rod said he'd received a lot of calls inquiring as to who I was. He told me the many complimentary responses he'd given them. Later, out on his front porch, he confessed his love for me and asked if I loved him. He wanted me to move in with him.

I told him I loved him but that I was not in love with him. I felt his huge heart sink through the porch floor. Was I so incapable of receiving love that I just couldn't tell who was good for me? Or did I just know who I was not good for? Was it really that or was I just choosing drugs over life? The depth of the rejection cut through him like a knife. I don't think he was used to it, especially from young would-be starlets whose lives he could rescue or make big. But at least I loved him enough not to use him. And I didn't pretend I was in love with him when I was not or perhaps I didn't know I was.

After that, I had a brief affair with a cute curly-haired Israeli named Shlomi. He, like most, had served in the Israeli army. At war, he had been blown off a ship and treaded nine hours in the cold waters until they rescued him. He used his underwear to make a tourniquet for his arm badly mangled by the wound he had sustained.

I admired his courage and his resilience, but I was not in any way in love with him. Imagine my surprise when I turned up pregnant. My diaphragm had never failed me before. It could be because I thought that since I was on my period, I didn't need the spermicidal cream. Be warned, ladies, you can get pregnant on your period!

When I found out, he was off on a cruise somewhere. It was then that I went to see Rabbi Hier. He was the only rabbi I knew. I told him that I wanted to convert to Judaism. He examined me momentarily from across his desk and then asked me, "Tell me what is your relationship with God?"

I got up, walked over to his desk, picked up his phone, and put it to my ear. I daresay no one ever answered him that way before. I explained to him my predicament. I was carrying the child of an Israeli soldier. I knew that without my conversion the child would not be accepted in either world—not Israel nor here. He said he had never heard such reasoning before. People had come to him wanting to convert for intellectual reasons and some for emotional reasons but never for this reason. So he asked me to read two books, Herman Wouk's *This is My God* and *The Sabbath* by Abraham Joshua Herschel, and told me to come back if after reading those I still wanted to convert.

Herman Wouk's book told about his life as an Orthodox Jewish playwright who could not attend his Friday night openings. I was most impressed by one comment of his in particular, "One day you will be praying in the temple, in the shul, in the Beit Knesset, and suddenly everything around you will turn to light. At that moment you will know why you have prayed all of your life." Evidently, we shared a common experience.

Herschel's poetic vision of Shabbat as a chance to surrender to God also contained within it this gem: "According to an ancient legend, the light created at the very beginning of creation was not the same as the light emitted by the sun, the moon, and the stars. The light of the first day was of a sort that would have enabled a man to see the world at a glance from one end to the other. Since man was unworthy to enjoy the blessing of such light, God concealed it; but in the world to come it will appear to the pious in all its pristine glory".

I didn't have the heart to get rid of the child straight out. I was working eight-hour shifts in high heels at yet another German restaurant, The Dresden Room on North Vermont.

At night, on occasion, I would go to see Roni. He and Marin were shooting coke by then and I thought I'd try it too. Marin described it as being raped by the devil. It was an overwhelming rush that somehow made me feel dirty. Here I was reading about Judaism to convert for the sake of my child, and at almost the same time, shooting coke. I learned how to inject and how to give an injection painlessly.

I think I only did it once while pregnant, but that was enough. Before the end of my first trimester I lost the child. I saw in the ultrasound the sack was deflating and the cord pulling away from the wall of the uterus. There is no doubt in my mind that I was solely responsible for the loss of that child. And I grieved for him. The doctor said he could do a DNC or I could go through the miscarriage naturally. I chose to let nature run its course. The doctor tried to comfort me by kindly saying it's just nature's way of trying to be sure everything is in good order.

It wasn't until Shlomi came back that he confessed he had left with $80,000 worth of ill-gotten gains from the hair products he was counterfeiting and lost every penny of it gambling on the ship. I will never forget the all-pervading despair that filled my room as he told me this disturbing story. Our short relationship was well over. However, I had stumbled onto something new I wanted to do. I returned to Rabbi Hier and told him I wanted to go forward with the conversion. Soon my studies would begin with Rabbi Kelemer, the grandnephew of Herschel.

As for Rod, I would miss his friendship for the rest of my life. On the day they buried him, I waited on the side for the family to leave, and then I approached his grave by myself. I told him I treasured all the time we had shared together, I loved him, and I would always love him. There was no one like him. Rod Steiger was absolutely one-of-a-kind.

Chapter Fourteen – Zohar

"Hallelujah" was a cave-like nightclub that catered to an Israeli crowd. Hidden away under a large discotheque, it was owned by Pini Cohen and his lover Beatrice. Pini, a Yemenite, was an excellent entertainer and the leader of the local Sephardic community. His smile and his personality, particularly onstage, made everyone love him. He played six instruments, sang in seven languages and often had people dancing on the tables. Beatrice was a tough, shrewd businesswoman, as beautiful as she was brainy, and co-owner of the restaurant. It became the hotspot for Israeli entertainment and consequently a hub of its mafia.

Patty and Eli knew Pini and Bea, so they helped me get a job there. I wore whatever I wanted and was an excellent server, though I could get surly from time to time! No one got the better of me for long.

I remember one night two men were fighting by the bar. The volume increased with the violence until finally one man had a chokehold on the other's neck and was taking him down while everyone stood there watching. I was the only one who approached the two embattled men. With both of my hands I began to pry the one man's arm off the other's neck. When he looked up and saw it was a woman trying to stop him, he let go, came to his senses, brushed himself off, and apologized.

Then as usual, I retreated into the background. No one who had watched that scene ever quite got over it. The general alarm that a woman had stopped the fight sounded through the room. I had publicly revealed myself as a woman of immodest strength—too tough to handle and definitely off the marriage market.

Now the men in the community were interested in me for an entirely different reason. They sought me out for the wisdom that was my reputation. How to weigh that against the fact that I did cocaine with them? They poured their hearts out to me, these men, who had seen so much death and danger, laid their souls at my feet. My imposing certainty was a sexual turnoff for most, which helped them connect with me as a human being. I had somehow achieved their respect and disgust at the same time.

Beatrice trusted me enough to ask if I would pick up the keys to the club and go get something for her. I opened the club door, switched on the light, and my attention was immediately drawn to the man in a poster at the foot of the stairs. I felt my entire existence held by a photo, as I went gingerly down the steps never taking my eyes off him.

This gorgeous man in the poster drew me in as if he was wrapped around my bones. As I stood before him, I was shaking from the top of my head to my toes, trembling uncontrollably. It was Zohar Argov. Then I noticed he was wearing what looked like a wedding band and thought, thank God he's married! But Bea would soon tell me he was not. He did "belong," as Bea put it, to a rich older woman named Tootsie. She was a bleached blonde with a cute figure for her age but an emotional wreck.

So when Zohar came to town, Beatrice tried to enforce a strict hands-off policy. "Remember, stay away from him!"

"Don't worry." I replied.

"He'll be here any minute!" Bea said frantically.

Then suddenly Zohar arrived and walked directly towards Bea, stopping short when he saw me. He took the cleft of my chin between his thumb and fingers, then turning to Bea he said, "You see this? I love this!"

I blushed as we drank in the first glance of one another's eyes, then shyly we both turned away.

From the first night, the second, the next and the next, I tried acting as though I did not know he was there. Weaving in and out between tables, running around the restaurant, I did my best to ignore him. Yet there he was standing up on the stage, Zohar Argov, with a microphone held loosely in one hand, as he sang.

I only occasionally glanced at him from the corner of my eye when he was singing. Oh my God, his voice! The tones of his soul washed through me. I felt everything, including his agony. He sang from the roots of his heart, seducing his audience. He made them feel more deeply, and they loved him for it.

I don't know at what point I realized he was watching me too. I felt his eyes follow me around the room everywhere I went, every move I made. His voice pierced through my soul. And still I tried to ignore him. He sang every night that week and I was afraid to look at him.

Then one night at closing, Pini walked up to me at the bar, "Zohar wants to see you backstage."

I didn't ask what for or why. I put down whatever was in my hands and strode up to the stage assuredly, despite the trembling inside. I drew back the heavy velvet curtains and slipped through to the small dressing room where Zohar sat waiting for me. The moment I was in his presence, a deep calm came over me. I could see that he was relieved as well, that I came when he called me. It reassured him of his own sanity, 'I was right, she does feel me'.

Zohar was brilliant. He could easily have achieved a law degree or a PhD, but he wasn't among those chosen to be educated at such high levels—just a common Yemenite, they thought. He was an avid reader, possibly a surprise to many. He read the daily newspapers and would reference things from authors I was surprised he knew. He was a self-educated, self-made man, who spoke a little English. I spoke almost no Hebrew.

He beckoned me to sit in the chair next to him. Then he put his hand on my thigh as if to say, 'Stay, you're here now.' He looked deeply into my eyes with such an intense knowing. And I gazed back bravely without thinking. For a moment it was just that; we did not speak at all.

Then Zohar broke the ice, "I come with you tonight?"

I did not hesitate, "Okay."

He stood up abruptly. "Wait here, I'll be back in a few minutes."

"Okay."

I sat patiently for only a few minutes. He returned, apologizing for keeping me waiting.

"You drive," he instructed. We hopped into my old Audi and headed to my home in Beachwood Canyon.

"I do not live for the gold. And I know you. You don't live for the gold. You see me going around, talking with all the people. I don't love this. I have to do this; it's part of my job."

I told him how beautiful his voice was, "I feel you sing from your soul."

He just smiled. He knew what I meant. As we pulled up to my house, I could hardly believe he was with me, though I knew he would be. We were connected at the core, hence the ease that rose between us. Zohar was humble and unassuming as he entered my home, and we climbed the stairs together. He seemed pleased by my artsy little pad.

Then he pulled me towards him and he kissed me so beautifully, as if he had done so a million times before.

"Do you have music?"

"I have your tape."

"No, you listen to that when you alone."

"Ah, Beethoven? Chopin?"

"Musica, classica?"

Then he noticed the large picture hanging on the wall above my bed. "Who is this?"

"My Teacher."

"What did he teach you?"

"He taught me about the peace within, Shalom beefnim."

I ushered him over to the foam mat on the floor that was my bed. Stacked with pillows, it served as a seating area as well. There was also a Herman Miller loveseat from Cooper and a glass coffee table. Zohar made himself comfortable, lounging against the plush pillows while I got some glasses for the Remy Martin he had brought with him. The tabletop served as a good place to draw out a few lines of coke. He offered me some, pointing to the lines, "At rotsa?" ("Would you like some?")

"Ani, lo." Me saying no to coke was new, but I already loved him and I felt deeply that I needed to give my purest self to him. I sat next to Zohar, and he listened as I told him of the beauty I had found within me. Then I closed my eyes, enthralled by the music.

"You feel the music?"

"Yes."

"It's good." He nodded his head. "You good teacher for the people, but you no good teacher for yourself. Like me, I good teacher for the people but I no good teacher for myself."

I was in awe of his honesty and his astute perception. He smiled back at me peacefully. Despite the language problem, we understood each other clearly.

He said, "You know, you no understand eevreet, and I no understand angleet, but I understand you better than if you speak eevreet and I speak angleet because I look here (pointing to my eyes) and I listen here (pointing to his heart)."

Then he began to regale me with stories of his life—the ones I guess he figured would be important for me to know. He had been married once to a beautiful young woman named Bracha (meaning "blessing" in Hebrew). I always knew she was his first love and that he would always love her. She gave birth to his son, Gili, (meaning "joy"), and he was a joy for his father. He told me they had been divorced for some years now and that she had re-married.

Then Zohar told me, "A woman accused me of rape and I was put on trial." He paused for a moment to be certain that I understood him. "The judge asked me, 'Do you think you can have any woman?'"

Zohar did not get the point of the question, because he answered, 'Any man can take a woman; he need only know how.'

The judge's gavel came down faster than Zohar could realize his glib mistake. He sentenced him to three years, though he served only one.

After a beat I asked, "So did you sing in prison?"

"No, I prayed."

I nodded my head in silence, regarding him deeply, without judgment. The Chopin waltz finished playing.

"You have more music?"

I played Beethoven. Zohar was astounded, perhaps never having heard it before. "It's beautiful. I love this!"

I was touched by the way he drew me in so close to him and trusted me so deeply. I felt the purity of his intent. He gently turned my face towards him and looked into my eyes. I fell into his eyes, into his soul, into love.

"I never thought I'd see these eyes in this life," I whispered barely audibly. I had never connected to love that deep and clear. Looking into his eyes was like looking into a mirror that showed me the other side of myself. He wrapped himself around me with his long lanky body, holding me passionately in a wild embrace. I began to melt quickly and it scared me. I tried to stop. I got up and then paused for a moment on the edge of the bed with my back turned toward him.

He rose from the waist, bracing himself on one arm. He did not reach for me. He merely said, "Mah? At Hitler?"

Is he calling me Hitler? I wondered. Or was he making a connection between my behavior and Hitler? Was he asking if I was anti-Semitic? (He didn't know that I was a Jew any more than I did. That revelation would come later as a great and wonderful surprise!) Or was he saying only Hitler could be this cruel to turn one's back upon such a love?

I settled for the second possibility and turned towards him again. In a split-second he gathered me up in his arms, slowly undressed me and sweetly kissed each newly revealed area of my body.

Then he pointed to his pants and said, "Ten li hagora cheli" ("Give me my belt").

I crossed the room and picked up his pants.

He said, "Lo, hagora!"

It took a moment for me to figure out that he meant his belt. I took it off the pants and brought it to him. He put it down beside him and beckoned me to lay with him again.

He ran his hands all over me until there was no inch of me left untouched. Then he gently turned me over. I was fond of this position for insertion because I found it quite easy to come letting my clitoris rub against the bed with the thrusts.

Then suddenly I felt the crack of his belt on my back as he entered me. I felt immediate shock and awe. As an ardent student of kung fu, I was trained to take a great deal of superficial pain. Now with any thrust the whip might join it. Over and over again I felt the burn of the strap on my back. I clutched the sheets tighter with each lash. As he pumped himself into me, whipping me with his belt, we came together in utter ecstasy. Then Zohar wrapped me in his arms silently, protectively, as if he would never let anyone or anything harm me.

In the morning, I took him back to his motel room not far from the club. We had gone back to my place for the sake of privacy so no one would disturb us that night, like the jealous little Tootsie. I dropped him off, asking for nothing, no promises, no, "When's our next time?" Nothing. I headed straight for Patty's.

By the time I arrived, she had already heard from Beatrice, who had already spoken with Zohar. Zohar told Bea what had transpired between us the night before declaring, "She liked it."

Patty was thrilled to be the first to tell me this. I was mortified. Not only because my privacy, which I value highly, had been trampled on, but because I had given myself to him so totally and he had so quickly broken my trust. Was he suddenly afraid, thinking he needed to protect himself?

Patty tried to tell me that he was known for his violent behavior and many women would accuse him afterwards. Patty pressed on further.

"Let me see what he did to you."

"What do you mean?" I asked.

"Well, you must have some bruises, some marks," she insisted. I went with her to their guest bathroom and lifted my t-shirt so she could see my entire back. She gasped when she saw the strap marks like flames in red, blue, and purple from the lashes on my back.

"Oh my God, how could you let him do this to you?"

"I love him," I blurted out without thinking.

Then I clammed up, refusing to defend myself or allow her any further peering into my private life. There was no way that I could explain to her what I did not yet understand. This was between Zohar and me, even if the world thought they knew something.

That night at work I wore enough clothing to cover the marks but went out of my way to look as gorgeous as possible. Then I proceeded to ignore him again. Tootsie sneered and growled at me, but I couldn't believe word had gotten to her as well.

She cornered me in the ladies' room as we both primped in the mirror, "Well, I hear it was a hot night last night!"

I deflected her. "Oh yes! There were a lot of people in the club."

She flashed me a look of disgust and stormed out. Turned out Zohar himself told her he was with me to let her know it was over between them. It seemed everyone wanted to own a piece of him, the women as well as the men.

When it was nearly closing time, Zohar approached me privately. "You come to me tonight?"

"Ken." ("Yes").

He pointed to his cheek, and I gave him a kiss. Bea, Pini, and Tootsie were all standing around the bar when I went to get my purse. Bea handed me a check announcing, "Don't come in tomorrow night, we won't be needing you!"

**

After serving his one-year in prison, Zohar had been taken under the wing of Hofni Cohen, Pini's older brother and a man who was to become a great friend to me.

I don't know where Hofni first heard Zohar sing; I only know that he fell in love with him. Hofni was the godfather of the Kareem, the Tel Aviv neighborhood where the Yemenites lived. He was known for his big heart. He recognized Zohar's gift and wanted to help him. He started by giving Zohar a few lessons on how to present himself like, "Remove the keys from your belt loop" for starters.

Hofni bought Zohar a couple of pairs of pants and several shirts, suiting him up for the stage. Then Zohar recorded an album at the bahr VAHZ Club (The Duck Bar) with some of Israel's finest musicians. He took the cassette recording to Meir Reuveni's office in the bus station district of Tel Aviv. Meir told me one day that Zohar walked into his office and tossed the cassette down on his desk saying, "Here, listen to this!"

Meir admired his moxie but only after listening to the first song, did he agree to hear the rest. The next day he called Zohar back to his office saying, "Okay, I'll make 10,000 copies of this, and we will see how it goes."

A week later there were 100,000 black-market copies in the street! He was an overnight success!

Zohar was asked to sing at a concert given in honor of Sadat and Prime Minister Begin during their peace talks. It was held in an open-air stadium with 100,000 people attending. Begin and Sadat sat in front. Hofni said he had never seen anything like it—every woman straddling her man's shoulders, dancing to Zohar's songs. Now even the Ashkenazi world would stand up and recognize him! This night gave birth to his enduring fame. I had no idea at all how famous he was in his own country.

Zohar was staying in a small motel apartment rented by Pini for the entertainers. Zohar called it "Hotel Hallelujah". Having arrived before me, Zohar opened the door and nodded for me to come in, saying, "I was afraid you would not come back."

"I know."

He reclined against the pillows and patted the place beside him, beckoning me to sit down. I sat on the side of the bed, facing him.

"Why did you?"

"Why did I what?"

"Come back."

"I love you. I want you to give totally of yourself and I pray perhaps one day the bad will just run out."

Zohar regarded me quite seriously, considering before he spoke. "I think for women once a month the bad blood goes, but for a man it just stays."

"I'll wait and see."

Still looking as if trying to see into me. "I want you never speak of what we have, 'Ben o been akh'. You know what it means, 'Lo, mah ze'?" He pointed to me and then to himself.

"Between us?"

"Ken."

"Promise me."

"I promise you, as long as I am with you, I will never let them put you in prison again."

He drew out a few lines of cocaine, offered me some, and again I declined. Then he began to tell me more about himself. "My father was alcoholic. I don't want to be like him."

He picked up the bottle of Remy Martin from the nightstand next to him and took a long swig. I casually told him I had considered joining Mossad at some point in my life.

He was alarmed at the thought. "Mah, at killer? You want to die?"

Strange how a simple direct question can so quickly dispel an illusion.

"No," I assured him.

There was a moment of silence between us then he brushed his thumb a bit roughly across my cheek.

"Why do you wear this?" he asked, referring to my makeup.

"I think it looks good."

"Go, wash it off."

As difficult as it was for me to be seen barefaced, I did it. I washed off all my makeup, even my eyebrows. My natural brows are very faint, my skin is pale, my eyes are green, and my lashes are thick. As I never thought of myself as more than a bit pretty, it was disarming for me to sit back down and look at him, allowing him to see my real face.

He caressed my cheek gently, "It's you!"

He reached for me and then, drawing back, he tugged at my dress and said, "Take this."

I undressed in front of him, a little awkwardly as I was unskilled at stripping. Then I climbed into bed next to him. In seconds he was on top of me spreading my legs wide before him. Up came the belt. He began to whip me between my thighs, across the vulva, and against the clitoris. I stared him down barely wincing from the pain, and when I was soaking wet from within, he plunged his big fully erect penis into me, and we came profusely together again.

Then he laid his head on my breast saying, "You will not think I'm a baby if I rest my head here, like this?"

"I will never think of you as a baby," I said, holding him securely with what was left of my strength.

Dawn was bursting through the lightly curtained motel windows when he fell asleep, and I began to weep. I was thinking of my father and how he had prepared me to be someone who could take this. I told myself that it was just Zohar's darkness pouring forth and that eventually it would run out.

A few nights later Zohar asked me to pick him up at some guy's apartment in West Hollywood. When I arrived, there were a bunch of men standing around the living room, and in the kitchen people were surrounding a glass plate or bottle. I explained to the first guy I encountered that I was there to pick up Zohar.

Someone went to get him for me from a back bedroom down the hall. I was already a bit uncomfortable waiting there when a young woman, completely naked, came strolling through the kitchen. Knowing how the cocaine games go, she may have been doing it on a dare or in the pathetic hope of getting another hit.

Just when the scene was beginning to turn me on, Zohar was standing by my side. "Go! This place is not for you. Go! I will call you later."

He did call later, though not that night. Next time I saw him at the motel, he was strange. He asked me if I had gone to some guy's house. I did not know the guy, did not recognize his name, and had not gone anywhere. Who had told him what, I do not know. My protest that it was not true was met with a hard slap across the side of my head. No bruise, no swelling, just a blind spot in my vision for the next two weeks. A blood vessel had broken behind my eye by the force of the blow. It was the first and very last time he ever dared to strike me.

In the morning I got up, squared off, and started performing sets of kung fu, fiercely beating down an invisible opponent. I thought by making him fully aware that I was capable of fighting back but didn't, he would have to check something in himself. Would it still be exciting knowing your brutality was being absorbed, with no response? From then on, he began to protect me.

It was during this time in Los Angeles that Zohar went up to Vegas. He called Bea when he was down to his last

$1,500: "Tell Pini, send somebody with money."

By the time the guy arrived with more cash, Zohar had parlayed the $1,500 to $50,000 at the blackjack table. He was a master at the poker face. He continued playing until he was back down to $25,000, and then he walked away from the table. It was such a big deal in Israel that they wrote about it in the papers.

When he got home, he called me. It was the night before I was supposed to see my Teacher in Santa Monica. We slept for a while, then early in the morning I got up and began to get ready to go. At first Zohar took exception to my leaving.

He said, "You know if it was anyone else, I would not let you go, but because it is him, and I know you love him, I will let you go. But I want you to ask him a question for me. Ask him what is the apple that Eve gave to Adam? I think it was cocaine, because when I do it I become killer, and when I take le matah, I no killer."

I already knew the answer. The Bible says they became ashamed of their nakedness, so the apple was the mind! Still I agreed that if I had the chance to ask, I would.

I called my friend Magdalena to come get me, as we had planned on going there together. Zohar took the phone out of my hand. He wanted to talk to her to be sure that it was really a woman. He told her, "It's okay, you can come and get her. I know she loves him. And I'm going to let her go because he has the only face I have ever seen that shines like the sun, even in a picture."

I was surprised to hear him say this, as he had never mentioned that impression to me. When Magdalena arrived, she popped in to say hello and then off we went. We were among the first to arrive at the venue, so we decided to go around to the back entrance and see if we could come in and help. We were given the task of setting up the floor chairs. Then we went through the stadium, checking each seat and the area around it for any extraneous debris.

I had worked with Magdalena's husband at a restaurant called, Persepolis. It was there that we first met shortly after I had received the gift. She was a beautiful young woman of Greek origin with long dark brown hair, and she wore long flowing dresses that made her look like the vision of purity.

It wasn't until she was six months pregnant on Christmas Eve that she lost her first baby, dead in the womb. Then she came forth with the story of her life as a teenage junkie doing heroin in Harlem. She figured the baby had died from the poisons built up in her body over her past. More likely, it was her belief in payback and retribution. Meditation was her new high now.

She turned out to be a brilliant businesswoman. Acting as a secretary, she took a floundering flavored-sex oil business, whose doors were already padlocked by the marshal, and turned it into a multimillion-dollar company.

As Magdalena and I scurried around the hall, pulling gum off chairs and picking up wrappers from the floor, a calm came over me. Amazing, the comforting feeling performing simple tasks for a noble cause could bring. An effervescent excitement began to build, bubbling all around the nearly vacant venue like the pressure in a champagne bottle held back only by the cork.

All the craziness was left behind. I had only my love with me and the wonderful feeling of all being well with the world. The hall was emptied of almost everyone shortly before the main doors were opened, for security to do their final sweep. I knew this because doing security was my first opportunity to help out.

Of course, we were not armed. There would be no need. When the main doors opened, we would stand on either side and just look in the eyes of the attendees rushing through. There was an unmistakable understanding in the glance. You just knew, "Enter, enter, enter," waving them through like a river running to the sea. Before Magdalena and I were asked to leave the hall, I told her to drop some unnecessary garment on whatever chair she wanted to sit when we returned. I chose a middle side aisle seat about 12 rows back.

The Teacher walked onstage on time to the minute. Everyone stood up, applauding. A great thrill rushed through the room. I felt so relaxed in his presence that as he spoke, I often laughed. He was so funny, especially that day. I remember his simple stories and how he held absurdity up to the light showing how harmless illusion truly is.

He lightened my heart, helping me to see that the burdens were a choice, that peace in abundance exists within me, and that it is within me "where the mortal meets the immortal." Pure bliss, not a drug-induced high, just bliss borne of itself alone.

There was no way to deny my gratitude for having finally been given the key that opened the door to myself. So when the Teacher asked if there were any questions, my hand shot up in the air immediately. I was the first person he called on. As I stood up, I felt a powerful serge of energy. Confident that my heart knew what I wanted to say, I thanked him profusely for the gift. I told him what it meant to me, how it had truly saved my life, keeps saving it, and answers my deepest longing.

He was pleased that I was enjoying it and spoke on that subject a few moments.

When I returned to Zohar that night, he stood for several moments staring at me, taking in the energy and all that he alone could see. Something was different about me. I was in a glowing state of purity. He wanted to hear everything that was said, though I could remember very little. I told Zohar I had spoken with him but I had forgotten to ask his question. That was okay.

"What did you say? What did he say?" He longed to hear anything my Teacher had said, the way a thirsty man longs for water. When I had finished telling him everything I could recall, he sat thoughtful for a moment.

Then looking into my eyes, he said, "I want you come to Israel. You want?"

"Yes."

"You will love it. Come stay with me. I care for you."

Zohar turned his attention to a small folded piece of paper on the nightstand, slowly pouring its contents onto a mirror. It was a brown powder substance I had never seen before.

"What is that?"

He snorted the two small lines he had made. "It's heroin. If you ever get addicted to this," he said calmly, "I kill you!"

Unflustered I said, "Don't worry, I don't want it!"

Zohar wrapped me in his arms, kissing my forehead. "Sometimes, when I take this I can't..."

"It's okay," I whispered, and buried my head in his chest. It was only two weeks since we met and all of this had already transpired.

**

Cooper and I had not yet formally broken up but we had been drifting apart. My resentment that Anna had him though I loved him had built to a breaking point. Not to mention my drug life on the side, which he suddenly became aware of by the tattling of a jealous friend. We actually had not seen each other since Zohar came to L.A. Then I got a call from him. Would I meet him at Spago's on Sunset for lunch?

When I arrived, he looked as gorgeous as ever, suited up so beautifully. I loved him so dearly. I will always love him. But now there was another love, a new love, a love that existed in the present and whose passion was burning out of control. I would have to tell him.

He ordered me a drink and said, "I have something to tell you. I am leaving Anna."

"I've fallen in love with someone else." I blurted it out almost simultaneously. The wincing pain that came across his face was heartbreaking. He knew he had lost me.

Sometime later I would get a call from his youngest daughter begging me to stop seeing him. I told her I hadn't seen him in a long time. It turned about to be a woman by the same name who owned a shop in the PDC that been after Cooper for years. All I know is that later he married her.

Years later, at a particularly vulnerable time in my life, I heard from him. He was retired and living in Palm Springs. He wanted me to come and see him. For so many foolish reasons, I did not go to him. Decades later while walking through a Gelson's parking lot, I saw the Speedster. I walked around it several times. I felt his mark on it. It was still nearly perfect, with its original red paint job and camel-colored leather seats. I stood there waiting for its owner to return. He finally did. It wasn't him.

I said, "Forgive me, but do you mind my asking where you got this car?"

"I bought it ten years ago from Bob Smith."

"Oh, I knew the original owner." Then sadly, I realized that he would never have given this car up, were he alive. For a moment I felt him near me again and I knew he knew that I still loved him.

**

It was nearly morning when Zohar and I entered the motel room arm in arm. I rushed ahead to put some water on for coffee in the kitchen. Just as I turned the flame on under the kettle, Zohar was there standing behind me. He turned me around by the shoulders and stared into my face, very serious, desperate to understand. "Tell me, when you look at me, what do you see?"

I smiled at him; he was so precious to me. "I see light pouring out of your eyes!"

He threw his arms around me and held me a moment as if he would never let me go. "Come."

I shut the stove off as he wrapped his arms around me and led me back into the front room. He sat me down on the bed next to him and emptied his pockets onto the nightstand. One guy after another had come up to him throughout the night, patted him on the back, and slipped something into his pocket. Opening up a couple of the packages, he drew corresponding lines of cocaine and heroin and snorted a little of each. Then leaning back he said, "You know, in Israel, all the girls have my phone number. They sit with their girlfriends like this--"

He picked up the phone, put it on his lap, and pretended to dial. "You see, I know Zohar Argov!"

Chiding him I asked, "All the girls?"

Zohar put the phone down and waxed serious again. "I want you to come to Israel, not as my wife. You come, stay with me. I care for you!"

"I know. I will come."

Then, too honest to lead me astray, he cautioned, "But, I like to fuck."

"You want to fuck? I feigned disinterest. "Fuck!"

Zohar was, I think, somewhat astounded by my seemingly endless composure. "Tell me what you want, Ben o been akh."

"I want us to have Shalom (Peace)."

"You never say me 'Shalom'!"

"I mean, I want to know the truth between us," I said.

"Gam li." ("Me too.")

**

Soon Zohar would be leaving, returning to Israel. Suddenly it was all happening so quickly we barely had a chance to say goodbye. I went to hear him sing on the last night. He took me backstage and he said, "I love you. I will never forget you!"

"You will not have the chance! I love you too."

We stood for the longest time holding one another, wrapped in the warmth of our mutual compassion, before the sad glance of parting.

As soon as I realized he was gone, I began to ache for him. After a month I felt I could no longer bear the pain of being separated from him. I was sitting with Patty in her living room looking quite morose.

"I want to go to him."

"So go."

"You know I don't have the money!" I protested.

"So call him and tell him, 'En kessef' ('No money'). Better yet, I'll call him."

Patty picked up the phone and dialed Zohar's number. I stepped outside onto the patio deck, closing the sliding glass door behind me. I leaned against the railing overlooking the pool below, as tears streamed down my cheeks.

Then Patty opened the glass door behind me shouting. "He wants you to come! Come talk to him. He's going to take care of everything!"

I rushed to the phone, overjoyed to hear my beloved's voice, to know he cared for me and that we would soon be together again.

I went to see my parents a few days before leaving at the new little home they bought for their retirement in San Dimas. I wanted to hug and kiss them, to say goodbye because I was going very far away and I did not know when I would be coming back. I confided in my mother that I was a little concerned about fitting in because Israeli women are so strong.

"I can't imagine there could be a woman stronger than you. You'll be fine!"

Compliments from her were rare, and so her confidence boosted mine. Then she expressed her fears, "I am worried about your safety. It's dangerous there."

"Don't worry Mother, I promise not to ride any busses! I will be well cared for and protected."

My father hugged and kissed me, making the sign of the cross over my forehead with his thumb as I was leaving. Mother did the same.

**

On the cab ride from Ben Gurion Airport, I was surprised to find the landscape of Israel so much like California. We were headed to the then small town of Rishon LeZion where Zohar lived. Alongside it was the small Yemenite village he grew up in called Shikun HaMizrah.

I arrived at Zohar's apartment with two large suitcases. A young man I did not recognize opened the door. He was Zohar's youngest brother Avshalom. Extremely kind and gentle, he bowed a little as he opened the door wide and reached for my bags.

"Zohar is not here. He is recording. He will be back soon."

With that he showed me to the second bedroom, placing everything carefully on the floor. I wandered around the apartment taking in the feeling of my new home. I walked out onto the porch that ran the length of the apartment and leaned over the railing looking up and down the street at my new neighborhood. All of the buildings were similar, somewhat prefab but sturdy with granite floors and large open rooms. Avshalom could not have been more congenial.

"At rotsa cafe?"

"Ken."

I picked up a cassette near the sound system. On it was a picture of that same poster I had first seen of Zohar.

Avshalom looked over my shoulder and pointed to the ring on Zohar's finger. "You see this? I bought that for him!"

It was gold and studded with diamonds. I couldn't imagine how long it must've taken him to save up enough money to buy it. The ring that I had once thought was sign of him being married was actually a gift from his little brother.

Just then Zohar arrived and rushed in to embrace me. With him was one of his best friends, a handsome man with salt-and-pepper hair and only one arm.

"This is my friend Haim. He will take you around when I can't. I trust him. He is a good man."

I reached with my left hand to shake his, avoiding looking at the stub that hung on his right. I learned later that he had been in a tank when it blew up. The guy sitting next to him had died. Haim lost an arm and almost his leg. He was in the hospital nine months recovering. He left the hospital a heroin junkie, the price of pain.

Zohar had not served in the Army. He told me he was a conscientious objector. "Why should I kill the Arab? He is my brother. Well, maybe not my brother but my cousin!"

Zohar motioned for me to join him on the sofa, patting the space next to him. "Come, sit, you home now." Then he suggested, "You want to shower?"

I got up and went into the bathroom, but before I had a chance to close the door Zohar was doing it for me. I undressed and got into the shower, turning the water on. Zohar undressed and followed me in. He lifted me up from behind and entered me immediately as I braced myself against the shower wall. I was trembling when he finished and left me alone in the bathroom. I waited a while attempting to compose myself before going out. It was so hot and humid, even after drying off I was damp before I could get my clothes on.

As I was arranging things in my new room, Zohar came in to see me. "Come, I want to rest with you before work."

He laid with me on my bed, nestling his head on my breast. That night, after Zohar left, Haim came back to take me to a nightclub in Jaffa called "The Caravan" where Zohar was performing. I was a little surprised to see the opening act included semi-nude couples dancing, or shall I say rubbing against each other sexually on stage.

I was uncomfortable but it was only one act I had to sit through before Zohar was standing there to sing. Zohar announced something into the microphone in Hebrew, so I did not immediately understand why the entire audience had turned to look at me.

Haim leaned across the table to tell me, "He said he wants to dedicate this song to his angel. That's you!"

I blushed as Zohar sang "Eleanor." Later, at Zohar's instruction, Haim took me to a wonderful little bar on the beach that served calamari. We drank shots of Russian vodka and ate two plates of the finest calamari I have ever eaten. The first was sautéed in a garlic herb sauce and the second in a delicate marinara. Both were cooked to perfection!

I was intrigued by the beauty of it all on the beach in a new land but under the same moon. I left Haim sitting there and went running down to the sea in my lovely white chiffon dress that floated with the breeze as I danced along the shore.

Suddenly I heard someone calling me in the distance. It was my dear friend Hofni. I ran to greet him. He said that in that dress I looked like a vision of a ghost coming off the sea and from that evening on he would call me ah-boo-lily (Arabic, meaning the boogie man or ghost of the night).

We were on that beach until dawn. It seemed everyone knew where to find us. It was there as the sun rose that I met Zohar's brother Amnon. He and Haim amused me with stories of the Yemenite world, dancing in their style against a backdrop of the sparkling sea.

On very little sleep, Zohar woke me, and we all headed back to the beach at Rishon. Zohar and Haim sat up front, Avshalom and I were in back. I watched in amazement and a trace of terror as Zohar demonstrated his unique method of driving, which consisted of perching on the bumper of the car in front of him and leaning on his horn until the car pulled to the side of the road, at which point he raced ahead to catch the next car and repeat the process.

We strolled along the pebbled beach. The sun blazed brilliantly on the surface of the sea, and Zohar was breathing deeply, relaxed at last. As we walked back inland from the shore, Zohar was suddenly surrounded by a swarm of little girls with pen and paper wanting his autograph.

One little girl said, "It's for my daddy."

This was the first time I got a picture of exactly how famous Zohar was, and his fame would grow until he became one of the most famous stars in all of modern Israel. His first manager, Ruveni told me, "In 50 years there will not be another like him!"

After bronzing me up a bit at the beach, Zohar took me to his mother's house where he had grown up. The family home was on a street called Marvad Ha-Ksamim, meaning magic carpet. His mother Yona Argov still lived there with at least one of Zohar's sisters and alternating brothers. It was a cinderblock and stucco building. The front room was painted a bright shade of lilac. It started as a one-bedroom home, with two additional bedrooms added on and a large unfinished hall on the side that was Zohar's bedroom but was now used as a communal bedroom or dining room to accommodate their large family. There was Jacob, Zohar's father's first son from his first wife, so Zohar's older brother. Then there were his mother Yona's children, the boys: Zohar, Betsauli, Amnon, and Avshalom; and the girls: Chochana, Abigail, Malka, Havi, and Mimi.

Yona Argov was a woman I will never forget. She had a sharpness in her glance that could rip right through you. From the moment I walked in her front door, she looked me up and down like, "Who is this my son brings here?"

Oh, but she was incredibly polite. She stared straight into my eyes looking to see, "Is she true?" Soon a smile came across her face, and her eyes shone brightly. She bade us to sit down, so excited to see her son again standing in her home.

Yona presented us with her cold, but highly spiced, whitefish in a broth of cilantro and serrano peppers. I had never attempted to eat anything that spicy-hot. I figured the faster I ate, the easier it would go down. Tears were streaming down my now reddened cheeks as I continued to swallow the hot Yemenite spices and Zohar watched in amusement. Yona continued to look me over for any sign of insincerity. Just as I got down to nearly the last spoonful, there was Yona, adding another ladle to the nearly finished bowl. I suspect she knew, now that I think about it, but she and her son always enjoyed a little amusement.

Later that night Zohar and I entered his darkened bedroom. I undressed silently and slipped under the covers. Zohar reached into the drawer and retrieved two straps. He motioned for me to lay at the end of the bed, took my arms and tied each wrist to the bedposts. I watched as a tear rolled down the silhouette of my beloved's face.

When he finished and untied me, I was unable to move. Not only was he almost too large for me to contain, but he had been pounding himself into me for hours pressing my thighs wide open as far as they could go, whipping, slapping, and lunging himself into me.

Zohar stared at the ceiling. "Go, fix yourself."

"I can't move."

When I was finally able to get up, I did so carefully, not immediately able to feel my legs. A deeper question burned in me as I mopped myself up. I could feel that something had happened to him to cause this behavior. In my arms, I could feel his history like an impression made upon me.

It was as if I knew without a word spoken exactly what had happened to him. And so, upon returning to bed, I decided to ask him straight out in the softest, most compassionate voice possible. "Can I ask you something?"

His immediate response was very serious, definitive, and delivered in a low tone. "No!"

One day the only person who knew for a fact what had happened to Zohar would brazenly confess it to me.

I was there less than a week when Beatrice called to tell me that Tootsie was on her way and I better get out of there. *Seriously?* I thought. I'm in my home, who does she think she is? Zohar, hours later, told me to pack a bag and said he was sending me to Eilat for the weekend. He would come later to sing. He put me in a cab and told the driver to take me to a specific hotel, where the manager would be waiting for me to arrive.

Did anyone think to tell me it would be a five or six hour drive down there? Of course not! I was being driven by a stranger and having to somehow relate to him throughout the long journey. As we went further south, I began to understand why it took Moses 40 years to get through the desert. The cliffs are so high and the passages so narrow, the entire layout is like a maze.

When I arrived, I was greeted by the manager of this modern hotel perched on the edge of some incredibly putrid water. There was an overwhelming smell of rotten eggs, due to the sulfur. The manager spoke some English and led me to the small room I was given right at the edge of the water. There were a few pieces of fruit in the room waiting for me.

The manager stepped in a moment to talk with me, as if he was interviewing me for a job. He told me I was welcome to stay there as long as I liked, provided I was willing to work. I could be a waitress if I liked. There were many girls who worked there that came from other countries like Russia. I said, "Excuse me but I live in Rishon with Zohar, and I'm not staying here. Isn't Zohar supposed to come and sing here this weekend?"

"No. Zohar is not coming. Not this weekend anyway."

"You're joking?"

"No."

"I'll be leaving in the morning."

I was out early on the first bus that would get me back to Rishon. It wasn't until we were far into the desert that I remembered my promise to my mother, that I would not take any public transportation while in Israel. It's strange, but I took a little comfort knowing that if anything did happen to the bus, the perpetrators would pay a heavy price in retribution.

When I returned to Zohar's home, there was no sign of Tootsie.

"You did not like Eilat?"

I said no and nothing more. Zohar was getting ready for another night of performing. He was meticulous about his appearance. Tall, thin, and elegant he would turn around several times before the full-length mirror that hung on the back of the front door, carefully tucking in his shirt, pleating the excess fabric in back and on either side for a snug fit. On stage his voice alone moved, as he stood straight and still like a statue.

Zohar approached me in the hallway and put his arms around my shoulders. Haim was in the living room waiting. "I am not coming home tonight. I want to go with someone."

I caught his meaning and pushed him away. "Don't touch me!"

I went into my room and closed the door. Zohar opened the door and found me sitting, ready to meditate. He called over his shoulder to Haim, "Come here."

Haim got up and looked as Zohar pointed to me sitting there. "You see this? I love this!"

Zohar was very fond of telling any room full of people, "Shut up and listen to her!" Then he would turn the floor over to me to tell them all about the gift. I was constantly studying Hebrew but extremely limited so I would speak half in English and half in Hebrew, yet they understood me. The truth drops directly into the heart. Its message is delivered by a feeling beyond words.

Though they listened at first only at his command, their faces showed they were grateful for what they heard. I saw that people could be mesmerized by the very sound of the Truth. Throughout these years I often felt compelled by the experience itself to speak of it. Sometimes those who listened to me speak of this wondrous peace attributed it to me. They marveled over the feeling emanating from me that stirred them. The room would fill up with the glistening air of hope. There were smiles all around, and all else was momentarily forgotten. Though I knew the beauty that I spoke of was my true self, I struggled with the multilayered fabric of the ego ever attempting to choke it out of me.

Later that night I came home drunk, only to find a woman, still fully clothed, standing in Zohar's bedroom. As I entered his room, I pulled off my blue silk dress over my head and standing in a full pink slip I began screaming at the woman. "Get out! Ani bahbyat! At Lo bahbyat! Get out!"

The woman was rather amused by all this and began laughing long and wildly, as I jumped into Zohar's bed defiantly. Zohar at last came to the rescue, escorting the woman out and calling her a cab. When Zohar returned to the room, he sat beside me softly. "What happened to you? Did you drink?"

I nodded, sobbing, as he rocked me to sleep in his arms.

I woke long before Zohar and scurried around the house performing my womanly duties. Later that morning he came looking for me in the apartment and gently led me by the hand to his room. He stood there facing me quite seriously as the morning light pierced through the bedroom shades.

"I want you to know, I believe what you say. I know it is the Truth, it is Love, it is God, but I don't want this. I want everything that is bad."

I was all at once happy and dismayed. Happy because he knew and perplexed at the thought that he did not want it. Zohar had finally managed to say something that I might never have understood without my own mad march toward death.

When I next saw my Teacher again, he said there was even a guy who said, "I know this is true, but I do not want it." I was sitting really close to center stage, about six rows back. I couldn't prevent myself from throwing my hands up in the air as if to say, "Well?"

After a beat he said, "I don't know what to say to that guy."

Early one morning, when I was the only one awake in the house, I entered the bathroom and was appalled to find a thick ring of scum around the inside of the tub. I entered Zohar's room only to find him asleep with a beach girl lying in bed next to him. A "beach girl" meant a young woman with no real home, no place to lay her head. At first, I just closed the door, and then I reentered the room walking around to the side of the bed where the girl was and woke her gently, careful not to disturb Zohar. I was quietly fuming as I led the young girl into the bathroom pointing to the mess, "Ma-ze? ("See this?") Clean it!"

She did not understand English but she got the message and obediently did as she was told. I paced around the apartment totally distraught at first and then I experienced a change of heart returning to the young woman in the bathroom.

"Come. Are you hungry? You want to eat?"

The poor little lady timidly followed me into the kitchen. I fixed her some coffee and breakfast, and we sat at the kitchen table together talking. She was 21 years old. We were communicating. There were key words we understood, and more importantly, there was something that flashed between our eyes.

We confessed to each other that we had strange memories of the camps in Europe. This seemed odd for a young Yemenite girl, because the Yemenites were not touched by this and mostly do not have the same scary memories. I marvel at how far communication can go without understanding much of the language!

Yona came later that morning around the time she knew Zohar would be waking. I think it pleased her that I was interested in learning Yemenite cooking. That morning she showed me how to make shakshuka, a wonderful stew of fresh chopped tomato, onions, and green peppers including serrano with cilantro in which eggs are poached. It is delicious and healthy too! She taught me to make Yemenite chicken soup as well. I can still see her smiling brightly, her eyes glistening each time she could do something for her wonderful son Zohar.

Zohar had taken my passport for "safekeeping" when I arrived. It was returned to me each time I went into town and taken back when I arrived home. I don't remember exactly the incident that led me to furiously throw the heaviest pieces of furniture around in my bedroom. I do recall I was considering throwing the furniture out the window.

It seems Zohar had left Avshalom in the apartment to guard me. He was refusing to give me my passport, stating that he could not do so without Zohar's permission. I was furious and went into a rage. Avshalom tried to pursue me into my room. I physically threw him out, slammed the door, and shoved the bed against it. Then I exercised my rage on everything else in the room. (I think my sister Kate would call that "an anger exercise.")

When I was finally spent, I sat on the edge of my bed and gently wept. When I went out of the room to find Avshalom, he was angry and a bit afraid of me. He thought I would be in big trouble and said, "I'm going to tell Zohar!"

Avshalom was very dear to me, and I know he was fond of me too. Zohar often left him to protect me. He was to go with me wherever I needed or wanted to go unless it was Haim's turn. Once he heard me singing in the house. He was surprised that I had a good voice and asked me to sing for the other brothers as well. Zohar was awakened one morning by the sound of my voice as I sang to them. When the songs were finished, he called me into his room, patted the bed beside him, and asked me to sit. Then he said, "Listen. I only do one thing. Please don't sing."

That night while Zohar was working, Avshalom and I went into town. We went for a slice of pizza and a soda. Betsauli, another of Zohar's brothers, joined us there. Then Avshalom went up to a policeman on the sidewalk and asked, "What time is it?"

Instead of just answering him, the cop demanded to see his identity papers, knowing full well he would likely not have them on him. Avshalom proved him right, and the cop said, "Come with us."

The next thing I knew, he and his partner flanked either side of Avshalom, leading him to jail. Avshalom tried to tell me to stay back with Betsauli, but I refused to stand down.

I followed behind them, pace by pace, all the way to the station. It was quite clear to me that he had done nothing wrong and shouldn't be arrested. I'd heard a rumor that many in the Rishon Police Department despised Zohar because he was making $50,000 a week and blowing it up his face. They supposedly wanted and expected better of him. Many of them had known the Argov siblings since they were children, and it seemed that they sometimes harassed Zohar's brothers to get to him!

I knew nothing of this when I arrived at the police station, a breath behind Avshalom and the cops. I marched up to the officer at the front desk, whipped out my passport, and slammed it on the desk before him, demanding answers in my extremely limited Hebrew.

In my most commanding tone of voice just as they were about to take Avshalom back to a cell I insisted, "Ani rotsa ladat, mah carah! Ani rotza maveenah, mah carah, ackshave! La mah?" ("I want to know what happened! I want to understand what is happening now? Why?") I protested, pointing to Avshalom.

The officer looked over my passport several times, occasionally pausing to look up and to glare at me. I stared him down. Then he turned to the cop, who was holding onto Avshalom, and said, "Let him go."

The next moment we were bouncing out the front door happy and free. As we skipped down the steps, Avshalom told me, "You are ten men."

I was highly complimented but only said, "I couldn't let them take you like that."

Now, after the temper tantrum I'd just thrown, Avshalom likely felt threatened, hurt, and insulted. Zohar's brothers all knew I was into kung fu and each of them went at me, but none could even get near me any more than my own brothers could after my first six months of training.

It turned out Avshalom was wrong about Zohar being angry with me when he heard of my behavior. Instead he came to me kindly and with compassion. He asked if I was on my period. I was.

Zohar had promised never to curse at me. Until now he had kept that promise, but when I told him that my sister, Kate had offered to pay my way back to L.A. through Minneapolis, he cursed her and me with a phrase that is not translatable in any sort of polite company and never to be said to anyone who might understand it!

He followed me into my room where I had already begun packing and said, "Forgive me. I am a human being. Just a little human being."

My heart melted and a tear or two rolled down my face.

"I want you to have a good life. You will not have a good life with me. But stay, the people love you! I will find a place for you, and I take care of you."

"I cannot stay here without you. You are everywhere. Everywhere I go, I hear your voice!"

We looked into one another's eyes through the sadness, to the love that would forever remain between us. Surely love would not fail us, but would we fail it? Should I have ever left his side? I still don't know.

To Be Continued

Acknowledgements

I am Grateful...

To John F. Quinlan and Jeanette Blanche (Witkowski) Quinlan, my parents, for their love and individual roles in shaping my character.

To Ora Cummings, my agent, for her enthusiasm, kindness, excellent editing and genuine friendship.

To Ian Hooper, my publisher, for reading it, loving it, and giving it a chance.

To Sherry Weinstein for her watchful eye, considered comments and loving inspiration.

To Mark William Spradley, for his steadfast honesty and unwavering loyalty.

To Steven Whitney, for his professional advice and his extraordinary generosity.

To Kathleen Mary Quinlan, for her constant love and guidance.

To Raphael "Ella" Quinlan, my daughter, for all she has taught me about compassion, tolerance and Love.

And finally, to Timothy Gallwey, my loving husband, for all that he is to me, my lover, my protector, and of course, my coach!

About the Author

Barbara Ann Quinlan was born in upstate New York and later raised in Southern California. For six years, she studied a radical form of eastern European theater; first with Leonidas Dudarew-Ossentynski at his studio in Hollywood and then at the Theater Laboratory of Jerzy Grotowski, in Wrocław, Poland.

Her studies included No and Kabuki Theater, ancient Chinese resonator techniques for the voice, Thai Chi and Chi gung, among countless other exercises aimed at breaking down one's resistances in order to develop the actor as a superhuman; capable of performing far beyond the normal human range.

Barbara wrote her first poem at five and has kept numerous journals. She studied French in Paris, Spanish in school and Hebrew in Israel. Throughout the years, she has used her knowledge of Chi gung to perform energetic healing.

After spending ten years traveling as the executive assistant to a well-known author who gives seminars around the world, Barbara now dedicates herself to the joys of life itself, her family, her friends and her writing.

Made in United States
North Haven, CT
07 October 2022

25165585R00075